PENGUIN SPECIAL S270
The Devolution of Power:
Local Democracy, Regionalism and Nationalism

John Pitcairn Mackintosh has been Labour
member of Parliament for Berwick and East Lothian
since 1966. Born in 1929, he was educated at Melville
College, Edinburgh, and at the universities of
Edinburgh, Oxford and Princeton. He was assistant
lecturer at Glasgow University in 1953–4, then
lecturer in history at Edinburgh University until
1961; he was senior lecturer in government at the
University of Ibadan, Nigeria, in 1961–3, and senior
lecturer in politics at Glasgow University from 1963
to 1965. He was professor of politics at the
University of Strathclyde in 1965–6. His previous
books are *The British Cabinet* (1962; revised in 1968)
and *Nigerian Politics and Government* (1966).
J. P. Mackintosh and his wife live in Edinburgh.

J. P. MACKINTOSH

The Devolution of Power

LOCAL DEMOCRACY, REGIONALISM AND NATIONALISM

PENGUIN BOOKS
in association with Chatto & Windus
and Charles Knight & Company

Penguin Books Ltd, Harmondsworth,
Middlesex, England
Penguin Books Inc., 7110 Ambassador Road,
Baltimore, Maryland 21207, U.S.A.
Penguin Books Australia Ltd, Ringwood,
Victoria, Australia

First published 1968

Made and printed in Great Britain by
C. Nicholls & Company Ltd
Set in Monotype Plantin

Contents

List of Maps

Chapter 1
The Weaknesses
of Local Government

Why should the words 'local government' induce a sense of boredom in even the most politically interested citizens? At times situations outside Whitehall can arouse intense passions. Scottish nationalists have whipped up enormous enthusiasm for a cause which, in U.K. terms, is essentially a problem of governing one part of the country. The attempt to abolish Rutland County Council produced a vigorous response; while accusations of corruption can rush a mass of reporters and television cameras to such an unlikely place as Bognor Regis.

Part of the answer is that local government is often defined simply as the powers and activities of the existing county, borough, and district councils and these are complicated, highly circumscribed and apparently of no great significance. Local government of this kind will only interest those who have settled in a locality, whose horizon is limited by their existing occupation, their present home, and for whom matters of local precedence and local facilities loom large. In any case, to understand such questions would appear to require endless work following the activities of slow-moving committees and the intricacies of legislation and of statutory orders which are hard to locate and understand.

This is a very limited view of local government. It underestimates the difference local government can make even in its present form. There is an atmosphere, a persona about cities such as Coventry or Glasgow, a feeling that they are governed in an enlightened or an old-fashioned way. Those living in the best-run counties have advantages, particularly in specialized services such as care of the mentally handicapped or nursery education, which the less capable, poorer or less enlightened councils do not offer.

Apart from the existing structure of local government, to ignore or write off all but the central departments of state would be to exclude the mass of governing bodies which have been set up outside Whitehall, bodies which are given limited areas of operation and are neither part of the central machine nor of the series of local elected councils. Sometimes collectively described as 'intermediate government', these boards, commissions and bureaux exercise important and interesting functions.

For example, a regional hospital board has a definite task of obvious value and there is competition to be appointed as a member. Within the professions or occupations concerned, the Forestry Commission and the Arts Council are respected, while a really efficient Countryside Commission or a statutory Tourist Board could do much to encourage the development of recreational facilities and holidaymaking in Britain. It was thought by many in the north and west of Scotland that the Highland Development Board represented the last chance to preserve something of the life of the area; there was great interest in the Board and the ablest and most active public figures in the Highlands were anxious to be nominated for it.

On the other hand, it must be accepted that the public has shown less and less interest in local government. Of the 22,739 seats open to election in England and Wales and the 3,148 seats in Scotland in 1967, only 11,822 and 1,176 respectively were contested. Moreover, where there were contests, it became evident that the electorate had not the smallest interest in the record or capacities of the local council as a whole or of individual councillors. The elections were treated almost entirely as a method of commenting on the performance of the Labour Government. Good, efficient, experienced councillors fared no better than the incapable and, in some places, candidates were returned who not only had no notion about local government but had openly claimed that they were standing simply as a demonstration against the Government in power in Westminster.

It is sometimes claimed that the low turnout at local elections is really an indication of contentment and maturity; by not going to the poll, the elector is demonstrating that he is satisfied that the local government meets his needs, while fierce contests would mean unpleasant local divisions. This argument cannot be taken very seriously as it suggests that the perfect democracy would be one where no elector bothered to vote at all. Abstention is more likely to be due to a feeling that the difference one type of council can make as against another is small; it may owe something to ignorance of the issues involved, something to lack of local pride and a consequent disinclination to make the necessary effort.

In local affairs, the public does sometimes become deeply concerned about its rights, amenities or services, but it is hard to translate these bursts of feeling into a distinct and positive interest in local government in that area. There was irritation far beyond Essex, for instance, at the handling of the decision to build a major airport at Stansted. The problem of how best to control the police is always leading to controversy in one city or another, while the attitude of individual authorities to the organization of secondary education can arouse intense passions. The trouble is that an eruption of feeling on one of these issues does not lead to greater involvement in local elections or the emergence of more and better candidates. The emphasis is always on changing a specific decision or removing some infringement of private rights without any clear idea as to who was responsible, how to alter the situation or why it is worth having better local administration. For all these reasons it is hard to maintain that local government is in a satisfactory condition in Britain today, but it is important that the reasons for its weaknesses should be analysed so that appropriate remedies can be prescribed.

The Weaknesses of Local Government

A. Electoral. Looking purely at the existing pattern of local government, in England and Wales, there are:

58 County Councils   82 County Boroughs

270 Non-county   473 Rural District   535 Urban District
      Boroughs   Councils   Councils

About 7,500 Parish Councils

As has been said, of the 22,739 seats vacant in the 1968 elections (county councils are elected every three years, borough councils have a third of their members elected annually) only 11,822 were contested and there was a 40 per cent poll. In Scotland the structure consists of:

31 Counties   4 Cities

21 Large Burghs   176 Small Burghs   198 District Councils

In these councils in 1967, 1,176 seats were contested out of a total of 1,972 and there was a 46·6 per cent poll, so that throughout the United Kingdom there is clearly a lack of public interest in local elections and a dearth of candidates. The seats that were not fought either had an unopposed return or had to be filled by co-option. While it is true that some of those brought into local government by co-option do become involved in and even devoted to the work, it is still the case that the quality of elected members leaves something to be desired. The ablest trade unionists, busy men in industry or the professions, do not tend to come forward. Surveys have shown that while there is a wide scatter of occupations (from landowners and farmers to professional men, retail traders, unskilled workers and housewives) councillors are frequently somewhat elderly, have lived over twenty-five years in the one locality and are self-employed or weekly wage-earners (so that getting time off work is not a serious problem). Three councillors out of four say they were asked to stand, and the time taken by committee work, the slowness in reaching positions of influence (such as committee chairmanships) and the absorption with detail, tend to discourage the younger candidates. In general, local government has not produced men who are well known or who are regarded as national political figures (with the one possible exception of Dan Smith of Newcastle). It is not a training ground for national leaders in the same way as it is, for example, in Germany or the United States. In the former case, Konrad Adenauer and Willy Brandt were mayors of Cologne and Berlin while Kiesinger came from a *Land* or regional parliament. In the United States, a successful mayor of New York or an able state governor is soon talked about as a possible presidential candidate.

B. *Administrative*. There are several reasons for the weakness of existing local government units as administrative organizations, and they arise largely from the historical development of local government. The first is the distinction originating in the Middle Ages between town and country, a distinction arising from the different social development of the towns as compared with the countryside. The townspeople had money gained by trade and wished to be free from their obligations to the local aristocracy. The method they adopted to achieve this purpose was to buy their exemption by paying a fee to the Crown in return for a royal charter. These charters set out the privileges and immunities to be enjoyed by all living within the town walls, privileges which usually included the right to self-government by a corporation chosen from among the citizens.

This distinction between the towns and the countryside was carried further in the nineteenth century. Then the pressure for electoral reform came first in urban areas, the result being the Municipal Corporations Act of 1835 which established a uniform system of councils to be elected on a property franchise in 178 out of the 246 towns then possessing charters. The Act extended the same rights to any other urban areas which the government decided to incorporate. Meanwhile the countryside remained under the influence of the aristocracy legally embodied in the powers of the Justices of the Peace, who combined enforcement of law and order with local administration till 1888, when elected county councils were created.

The different rate of democratic development confirmed the distinction between local government in towns and in the countryside, the result being that a county has always had an administration which, though it stretches across an area, has its fabric shot full of holes, each hole representing a self-governing county borough where the writ of the county council does not run. To add to the complications, in the further legislation on local government it was appreciated that smaller towns wanted some part of the self-government enjoyed by county boroughs, but that these communities had not the resources in population or wealth to sustain all local government services. As a result, they were allowed to elect councils which were given certain services to perform but the more complicated and costly services were still administered by the county council for what was described by the clumsy title of a 'non-county borough'. This arrangement produced a further complication in that such

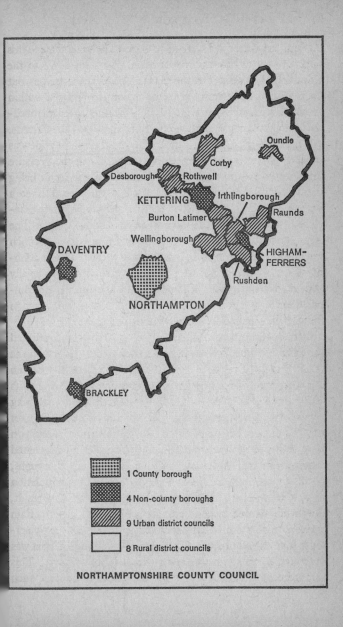

Oundle

Corby

Desborough · Rothwell

KETTERING · Irthlingborough

Burton Latimer · Raunds

Wellingborough

DAVENTRY

HIGHAM–
FERRERS

Rushden

NORTHAMPTON

BRACKLEY

1 County borough

4 Non-county boroughs

9 Urban district councils

8 Rural district councils

NORTHAMPTONSHIRE COUNTY COUNCIL

Local Government in an English County – Northamptonshire

The division of responsibility between County Council, Borough and District Councils. The County Council and the County Borough perform all functions except those given below in the listed areas.

The Four Non-County Boroughs	The Nine Urban District Councils	The Eight Rural District Councils
The Basic Services Housing Building Regulations Highways (unclassified roads and bridges only) Water Supply (unless by an incorporated body) General Sanitation including sewerage and refuse collection Burial and Cremation Street Cleansing Public Lighting Aerodromes Education – some delegated powers *Social Services* Public Health – some limited powers	*The Basic Services* Housing Building Regulations Highways (unclassified roads and bridges only) Water Supply (unless by an incorporated body) General Sanitation including sewerage and refuse collection Burial and Cremation Street Cleansing Public Lighting Aerodromes Education – some delegated powers *Social Services* Public Health – some limited powers	*The Basic Services* Housing Building Regulations Water Supply (unless by an incorporated body) General Sanitation including sewerage and refuse collection Burial and Cremation Street Cleansing Public Lighting Aerodromes *Social Services* Public Health – some limited powers

Amenities	*Amenities*	*Amenities*
Public Parks	Public Parks	Public Parks (mainly by parish councils)
Provision of Allotments	Provision of Allotments	Provision of Allotments
Civic Restaurants	Civic Restaurants	Civic restaurants
Public Libraries	Public Libraries	
Baths and Wash-houses	Baths and Wash-houses	
Rating and Registration	*Rating and Registration*	*Rating and Registration*
Rating	Rating	Rating
Regulative Duties	*Regulative Duties*	*Regulative Duties*
Food and Drug Regulations	Food and Drug Regulations	Food and Drug Regulations
Shop Hours Regulations	Shop Hours Regulations	Shop Hours Regulations
Weights and Measures		

towns had to pay part of the local taxes they raised to the county and were entitled to send some representatives to the county council to deliberate on the management of those services which the county provided for the townspeople. In the same way urban and rural district councils were constituted and allocated a more restricted group of functions. Finally a third tier of parish councils was recognized in rural areas and permitted a few very minor forms of activity.

The effects of this system in geographical terms is best seen by examining the accompanying map of a typical county, Northamptonshire, where the county council administers some services throughout the county except for the county borough of Northampton. Certain of its functions remain in the non-county boroughs of Brackley, Daventry, Kettering and Higham Ferrers, a few more in the nine urban district councils and rather more again in the eight rural district councils.

A similar chart for Scotland has only a two-tier system in the rural areas but the complexity of the administrative divisions remains.

A further reason for administrative weakness is that all councils in the same category have the same powers although they may differ considerably in terms of population, financial resources and therefore in the range of services they can provide and in the number and expertise of the staff they can employ. For instance, Rutland or Westmorland with populations of 27,950 and 67,410 (where a penny added to the local rates raises £3,401 and £9,420 respectively) are supposed to be able to provide the same standard of education and the same welfare services as Lancashire with 2·3 million people where the same extra penny in taxation raises £325,741. Among the county boroughs the range is from Birmingham with 1·1 million inhabitants and a penny rate of £204,450 to Canterbury where 32,770 people paying another penny produces £6,350. In Scotland authorities with the same type of function tend to

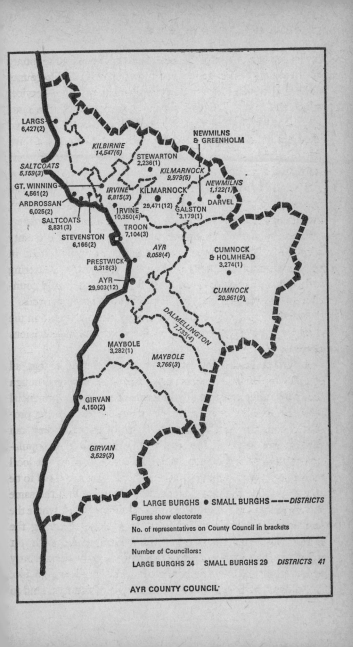

LARGS
6,427 (2)

KILBIRNIE
14,547 (6)

NEWMILNS
& GREENHOLM

STEWARTON
2,236 (1)

SALTCOATS
5,159 (3)

KILMARNOCK
9,979 (5)

GT. WINNING
4,561 (2)

NEWMILNS
1,122 (1)

ARDROSSAN
6,025 (2)

IRVINE
5,815 (3)

KILMARNOCK
29,471 (12)

DARVEL

GALSTON
3,179 (1)

SALTCOATS
8,831 (3)

IRVINE
10,350 (4)

STEVENSTON
6,166 (2)

TROON
7,104 (3)

AYR
8,058 (4)

CUMNOCK
& HOLMHEAD
3,274 (1)

PRESTWICK
8,318 (3)

AYR
29,903 (12)

CUMNOCK
20,961 (9)

DALMELLINGTON
2,733 (4)

MAYBOLE
3,282 (1)

MAYBOLE
3,766 (3)

GIRVAN
4,150 (2)

GIRVAN
3,529 (3)

● LARGE BURGHS ● SMALL BURGHS ---*DISTRICTS*

Figures show electorate

No. of representatives on County Council in brackets

Number of Councillors:

LARGE BURGHS 24   SMALL BURGHS 29   *DISTRICTS* 41

AYR COUNTY COUNCIL

Local Government in a Scottish County – Ayrshire

The division of responsibility between County Council, Town Council and District Council.

The Two Large Burghs – Ayr and Kilmarnock	The Fifteen Small Burghs	The Ten District Councils
These are independent of the county council for all local authority functions except education and valuation (and they are only represented on the county council for education and valuation matters). This means that they are independent of the county council for:	For all local government functions except those given below, the small burghs look to the county council (with small burgh representation). This means that they are independent of the county council for:	For all local government functions except those given below, the land-ward county looks to the county council (on which it is directly represented). District councils are responsible for:
Law and Order	*The Basic Services*	*The Basic Services*
Police	Housing	Maintenance of public ways and footpaths not on the county council's list of highways.
Civil Defence	Building Regulations	
Fire Service*	Highways (unclassified roads and bridges only)	
Remand Homes	Water Supply***	*Amenities*
Probation Service**	General Sanitation (including sewerage and scavenging)	Public Parks
		Physical Training and Recreation
The Basic Services	Clean Air	Entertainments
Housing	Burial and Cremation	Provision of Allotments
Building Regulations	Coast Protection	
Highways		
Town and Country Planning	*Amenities*	
	Public Parks	

General Sanitation (including) sewerage and scavenging)
Clean Air
Burial and Cremation
Coast Protection

Social Services
Child Care
Welfare of the Aged and the Handicapped
Public Health

Amenities
Public Parks
Physical Training and Recreation
Entertainments
Provision of Allotments

Rating and Registration
Rating
Registration of Births, Deaths and Marriages

Regulative Duties
Food and Drugs Regulation
Factories Regulation
Shop Hours Regulation
Weights and Measures
Cinema Licensing
Taxicab Licensing

Provision of Allotments

Rating and Registration
Rating

Regulative Duties
Factories Regulation
Shop Hours Regulation
Weights and Measures
Cinema Licensing
Taxicab Licensing

* The town councils of Ayr and Kilmarnock, with the Ayr County Council, are represented on the South-Western Fire Area Joint Committee.

** The large burghs of Ayr and Kilmarnock have been combined with the County of Ayr for purposes of the Probation Service.

*** The small burghs of Irvine, Stevenston, Saltcoats and Kilwinning and Ayr County Council constitute the Irvine and District Water Board.

be smaller, the largest county being Lanarkshire with 597,554 (penny rate £63,105) while Sutherland, Peebles and Bute all have under 20,000 people and a penny rate in each case produces under £4,000.

Not only has the same function to be performed by organizations with such varied capacities but many of the units are far too small to provide the range of facilities now required by the electors. The evidence of the Departments of State to the Royal Commission on Local Government in England in many cases indicated the minimum population they considered necessary for the proper conduct of a service. This can be estimated because fewer people means insufficient material (e.g. certain numbers of children are needed before there are sufficient cases of the very deaf to merit special treatment) and because too little money means untrained staff and an inability to finance capital projects.

For instance, the Department of Education and Science estimated that the minimum population for an education authority should be 300,000; they did not want to argue that there was any ceiling figure but they considered that 500,000 would be about the optimum size. In this case 13 of the 45 English counties, 11 of the 13 Welsh counties and 27 of the 31 Scottish counties fall below the minimum population level. County boroughs also have to provide a full educational system and 70 of the 78 in England, all four in Wales and two out of four in Scotland have less than the basic figure of 300,000 inhabitants.

The Home Office recommended that before local government units could conduct adequate children's services, there should be a minimum population of 250,000, while the Ministry of Health said 'we doubt if any authority with a population of less than 150,000 is capable of developing the full range of services effectively and economically' and they indicated a preference for a figure of 200,000 to 250,000.

Modern physical and land use planning also requires large

units and the recommendations of the Steering Group for the Buchanan Report, *Traffic in Towns*, under Sir Geoffrey Crowther, simply stated that 'a programme for the modernization of Britain's cities could not be carried out by the present machinery'. The Steering Group argued that it would be necessary to plan on the basis of urban regions taking in 'the whole of the surrounding catchment area, going at least as far out as the "traffic watershed" or limit of car-commuter travel'. The Ministry of Transport in its recommendations to the Royal Commission was almost as sweeping, putting the case for 30 to 40 major transport authorities instead of the present 823 bodies responsible for highways and road safety, 382 traffic authorities and 1,190 parking authorities in England alone.

There is also the problem of the adequacy of second-tier councils. These councils are at present entrusted with housing and, while the English Ministry of Housing has found no close correlation between the size of authorities and their house-building record, the Scottish Office in their 1963 White Paper on *The Modernisation of Local Government in Scotland* (Cmnd. 2067) considered that adequate staff and continuity could not be maintained by a body representing fewer than 40,000 people. In this case, of the 1,190 housing authorities in England, 168 in Wales and 232 in Scotland, only 232 in England, 11 in Wales and 28 in Scotland are above the 40,000 mark, while 116 in England, 56 in Wales and 110 in Scotland are under 5,000 strong. Llanwrtyd Wells (510 inhabitants), Betws-y-Coed (770), Newcastle Emlyn (680), Inveraray (493), Tobermory (617), Lauder (590), Culross (507), and New Galloway (333), are all housing authorities. Thus when the Scottish Office recently circularized housing authorities asking for a 33 per cent increase in their five-year housing programme, one of these small burghs replied saying it was a little difficult as the programme stood at one house.

In addition to the variation between the sizes of authorities charged with the same function and the fact that many are simply far too small for the complexity of the services they have to organize, there is often a further weakness arising from the inappropriate extent of the authority's boundaries. This is not quite the same as being too small. Glasgow with a million citizens is big enough to muster an adequate planning staff, but the area is unsuitable, since Glasgow is part of a single conurbation on the Clyde valley where there are, in fact, fourteen separate planning authorities.

In general, the division between town and countryside already noted causes many problems. Residential suburbs have often spread outside the boundaries of a town so that many who use the facilities provided by the town do not contribute in rates to the cost of these facilities. The tight-jacket of old urban boundaries not only produces constant quarrels between borough and county councils but often means that cities cannot control their water supplies or plan their transport systems, as these may involve neighbouring authorities. To take another example, it is not easy to be precise about the most appropriate size or area for a police force but it was very unsatisfactory that till the recent series of mergers, a criminal seizing a car in the Midlands and driving fast in any direction for an hour was bound to pass through the territory of at least six separate police forces each using a different radio communication wavelength.

The result of the inappropriate nature of the areas covered has led, in the first place, to local authorities being empowered to set up joint boards for such functions as public health, port health, water supply, sewerage, burial, police, harbours, tunnels and airports. While this may seem to be a reasonable solution of the problem of areas, a joint board may create some special problems of its own. For instance, it is the joint board which draws up any plans for expenditure but it has then to call on the member authorities to foot the bill and some of them may object. To meet this difficulty joint boards will not proceed if members representing one authority are strongly opposed, but this gives a veto on progress to the most backward-looking member. Finally, the sense of popular control is remote enough in the case of elected local authorities but it virtually disappears when these bodies unite to create a joint board.

A second effect of this problem of area has been the creation of the statutory boards and commissions already referred to. Some have been set up precisely because the local authorities were not thought to be capable of continuing with a service, as when local authority hospitals were removed in 1948 and handed over to the newly created regional hospital boards. Others were formed when the authorities failed to make use of powers given to them. For example, county councils and county boroughs have wide planning powers. The central government urged local authorities to use these powers to designate areas of high amenity value, in order to control development in parts of the countryside specially suitable for sport and for holidays. After ten years of circulars and exhortation only a small minority of the councils had taken action, while the need for ski resorts in the Scottish Highlands, and for national parks throughout Britain for recreation, camping and walking, became ever more evident. Eventually the Government decided it could not let these matters drift and in 1967–8 passed Bills setting up Countryside Commissions in England, Wales and Scotland to perform these functions.

Ad hoc bodies of the kinds indicated can take many forms. They may be groupings of local authorities; they may be set up by statute or by royal commission to execute certain schemes or make certain investigations; they may have permanent advisory duties; but whatever the form or purpose, they have proliferated in recent years. The numbers and variety of these bodies make them hard to list: a parliamentary question on the number was returned unanswered on the grounds that there were so many and the decision of which to include and which to omit was too difficult. In general, wherever there are special administrative problems, this method is adopted, particularly when the local authorities lack the resources in staff or manpower, or where their boundaries are too narrow. For these reasons, there are a large number in the depopulating areas of rural Wales and the Highlands of Scotland.

'Ad Hoc' Bodies with responsibilities in North and Mid-Wales

Welsh Tourist Board	Area Gas Board
National Parks Authority	Arts Council
Two Water Resources Boards	Sports Council
Five River Boards	Hospital Board
Mid-Wales Industrial Development Association	Eight Agricultural Executive Committees
Rural Industries Commission	White Fish Authority
Development Commission	Land Commission
Countryside Commission	Nature Conservancy
Forestry Commission	Ancient Monuments Board
Merseyside and North Wales Area Electricity Board	

'Ad Hoc' Bodies with responsibilities in the Scottish Highlands

Highlands and Islands Development Board (incorporating the Highland Transport Board)	Twenty-Four District Salmon Fishery Boards
	Area Gas Board
Crofters Commission	Commissioners of Northern Lighthouses
Three Agricultural Executive Committees	Land Commission
White Fish Authority	Nature Conservancy
Herring Industry Board	North of Scotland Hospital Board
North of Scotland Hydro-Electricity Board	Water Boards
Forestry Commission	Scottish Special Housing Association
Scottish Tourist Board	Ancient Monuments Commission
Red Deer Commission	Countryside Commission

While all these organizations were created to meet a need and many, no doubt, do good work, it is not surprising if the mere number of authorities, in addition to the county and borough councils, creates serious problems of co-ordination. Each has its own *amour propre* and has to be consulted, each can hold up change for a considerable period, policies may overlap and duplicate (e.g. there are three bodies concerned with tourism in the Highlands) and the total effect is that the citizens have no idea where to apply pressure in order to obtain a given change. It is some consolation to reflect that the collective fares of all the members of the Scottish boards on their visits to the Highlands are a further form of state sub-sidy for the uneconomic railway, aeroplane and steamship ser-vices, and if each member undertook to plant one tree per visit, it would go far to restore the ancient forests.

A final effect of inadequate size and inappropriate areas has been the extension of central government control and super-vision over those functions still ostensibly left to the local authorities. While this is intended to bolster up the weaker brethren, and often does do so, it can also be a source of weak-ness. Too much central control can slow down the process of administration, and makes the precise responsibility for a ser-vice unclear, thus leaving the elector bemused as to who is running what.

For instance, as far as most citizens are aware, county or county borough councils maintain schools and pay teachers. If there are any complaints, the person to go to is either the local councillor or the director of education. Yet in very many cases, these representatives or officials can shrug their shoulders and say that it is all the fault of the Ministry. This used not to be the situation. The old Board of Education set up in 1899 was charged merely with 'superintendence of matters relating to education', while the work was done by the local authorities. When its place was taken by the Ministry of Education in 1944 the latter had much more positive duties: 'to promote the education of the people', to ensure 'the progressive development of institutions', and 'to secure effective execution by local authorities under his (the Minister's) control and direction, of the national policy'. This can and at times has reduced local authorities to the status merely of agents of the central government with the right to alter the pace and adapt the form of educational developments to local conditions, but little more. The extent of the control is seen by the Ministry's own description of its duties in 1967. In addition to guidance by means of pamphlets, circulars and White Papers,

the Department sets minimum standards of educational provision; controls the rate, distribution, nature and cost of educational building; controls teacher training and supply and determines the principles governing the recognition of teachers as qualified; administers a superannuation scheme for teachers; arranges for the incorporation of estimates of local education expenditure in provision for general grant; supports financially by direct grant a limited number of institutions of a special kind; supports research; and settles disputes, for example, between a parent and a local education authority, or between a local education authority and the managers of a school.

It may well be wondered, after this list, in what sense education can be described as a local authority function. The same is true in many other fields such as health or redevelopment schemes, while in the case of major roads it has been thought better to alter the legal position so that it is now accepted that the responsible body is the Ministry of Transport, which will usually use the local authority as an agent to carry out schemes of road building or improvement.

Having noted these developments, the Committee on the Management of Local Government in 1967 reported that

there must be a fundamental change in the attitude to local government of the national authorities. The trend of recent legislation and the practice of government departments have been steadily reducing the discretion of local authorities and converting them into agents of Ministers and Whitehall. This tendency must be arrested and reversed; otherwise persons of the calibre required for effective local democracy will not offer themselves for election. . . . The national Government must give local authorities a larger measure of home rule.

These administrative defects mean that though local government does not grind to a halt, it is often slow, usually complex, with patches of positively poor performance and much mediocrity relieved by occasional achievements. In general, it is a clumsy and out-dated system which could only have been produced by a long historical process and by a people who prefer patching old machines to devising new models.

C. Finance. Finance is another cause of weakness, since the freedom and sense of responsibility of an elected body is enormously increased if it has to raise the money it wishes to spend. Here again the structure of local government is a problem in that some units have either few resources or serious needs or both (e.g. miles of road in remote rural areas or a mass of slums in a Victorian mill town) and they may therefore find it very difficult to carry out their duties. For example, the burgh of Glossop has a low level of wealth from which to pay local taxes (1d rate raising £1,847) though much of the town consists of old and not very satisfactory nineteenth-century housing, while the London borough of Kensington and Chelsea can raise £101,700 by adding 1d to the rates.

Part of the problem is that since local services began as aids to property-owners (in the form of paved and lit streets, water and sewerage pipes) the traditional tax is a rate upon property values. The disadvantages of such a tax are numerous. From the point of view of the local authorities rates as a tax lack buoyancy. Incomes have tended to rise in modern times so that the same level of income tax produces a steadily rising yield where-as, apart from infrequent revaluations, the only way of getting more out of rates is to raise the level of the tax. It is also un-popular from the point of view of the taxpayer, because till 1967 it had to be paid either yearly or half yearly (rather than as a few pence on each packet of cigarettes) and because it is regressive. Thus, a family of three earning under £676 a year pay 3 per cent of their income in rates as compared with 2·1 per cent by those earning around £2,000 a year.

Thus, as a source of revenue, the tax is unresponsive to changes in general levels of wealth and unpopular. Also it does not have to be paid by income-earners who are not house-holders, though they may make as great use of civic services as the ratepayers. It is possible that successive governments have retained this method of raising local revenue precisely be-cause its inflexibility and unpopularity imposes a severe limit on how much the local authorities can spend. Held on such a tight rein, councils have had to turn increasingly to the central government for grants, thus giving Whitehall a greater right to supervise their expenditure.

Sources of local government current expenditure. Selected years, 1938–1963 (in percentages)

	Rates	Other income	Central gov. grants
1938	43·2	27·9	28·9
1952	41	18·4	40·6
1955	39·2	20·3	40·5
1960	39·2	21·1	39·7
1963	39·3	20·8	40

The importance of local government as a user of national re-sources is shown by the fact that in 1967 its capital expenditure in England and Wales totalled £1,570 million, current expenditure amounted to £3,961 million (16·3 per cent of gross domestic expenditure), and there were 1,900,000 paid employees of local authorities.

In an attempt to help local government fulfil its tasks but at the same time to keep a close control of local expenditure, the central government has devised an exceptionally elaborate formula set out in the First Schedule of the Local Government Act, 1966. Government grants under the Act fall into two categories, the rate support grant and specific grants. The former has three elements described as 1. needs, 2. resources and 3. domestic. The needs element is calculated by taking a prescribed amount of money and multiplying it by a series of factors based on population, those under 15, those under 5, those over 65, density of population per acre, sparsity of population per mile of road, ratio of school children to general population, road mileage and a mass of shared costs. The resources element is worked out by taking the product of a penny rate for the whole of England and Wales; if the product of such a rate in the local authority in question is less than the U.K. average rate for such a population, some grant is payable. The amount of the grant is fixed so that it bears the same proportion to the total expenditure of the authority as the proportion the local yield of 1d rate bears to the U.K. yield of 1d rate, with careful provision to see that the local authority is doing all it should in the way of rate-borne expenditure. The domestic element is intended as a relief for domestic ratepayers and is fixed at a certain number of pence in the pound reduction for householders (5d in 1967–8 and 10d in 1968–9).

The second category of grant, as has been said, is that of specific grants for which twenty services qualify, some of the services attracting two or three different types of grant. For instance, the employment of blind and severely disabled persons can claim central government aid on three counts; an annual capitation grant not exceeding £300 per person, contributions of up to 75 per cent on approved capital expenditure, and payments of up to £165 a year towards the approved cost of training handicapped persons for employment. Other functions that can be grant-aided include expenditure on clean air, coast protection, roads, police, probation, water supplies, slaughterhouses, small holdings, welfare foods, and youth employment; there is special aid for areas with immigrants and to help with the cost of rate rebate schemes.

Local authorities may also borrow to finance capital expenditure and in many cases authority to borrow has to be obtained from the ministry concerned (Education and Science if it is a school or Transport if it is a road). As a result, finance is one of the main reasons why departments in local authorities tend each to look to the relevant Whitehall Ministry (or Scottish or Welsh Office) for direction rather than to their own council for overall control. Long-term planning is difficult when the deciding factor is 'consent' from the central government, a consent which may be withheld for reasons that have nothing to do with the needs or performance of the local authority. Over all there hangs the fear of the District Auditor's powers of inspection and surcharge on councillors. It is not surprising that the Committee on the Management of Local Government became 'convinced that the ... unfavourable financial position of ... local authorities is a major cause of the widespread frustration in local government'.

It is also a major cause of the widespread frustration with local government. The financial system limits any council's capacity to act in the general interest of its citizens, since rates are such an unpopular and unsatisfactory tax. Finally, the incredible complexity of the various formulae makes it hard for councillors, officials or electors to be clear about one of the most basic questions in politics: 'I want this done, but how much will I have to pay?' For instance, at a municipal election meeting in 1968 an experienced councillor standing for re-election said that he was in favour of his particular non-county borough building a specific number of new houses on one of the vacant sites. He said he realized that this would involve an extension to the town's sewage works and some extra road-building. When the comment was made: 'An excellent idea, but what will this put on the rates?', he had to reply that he had no idea. The houses would attract certain subsidies and so would part of one of the roads. Once the scheme was built, it would alter the rateable value of the town and thus affect the resources element in the grant. At the same time legitimate expenditure (e.g. on the sewage works) would have risen and this would affect the needs element. He could therefore only hazard a guess at the total result in terms of the cost to existing ratepayers, and when the Ministry of Housing and Local Government was asked the same question it could only give an estimate.

This was, however, a relatively simple case. In 1968 the Government published a two-volume report, *The Central Borders: A Plan for Expansion*. To prevent further rapid de-population of the central Scottish Borders, a most careful study was undertaken which proposed to build up the population from 76,000 to 98,000 by 1981. The Plan involved expansion of the existing small towns, the building of virtually a new town, major road improvements, the introduction of new industry and of many amenities. The area studied covered the entire territory of three county councils, parts of two others and included seven small burghs with their own councils. When the Plan was explained at public meetings, two questions were immediately asked. Given that at least ten local authorities were concerned, who was to co-ordinate them and actually carry out the plan? Secondly, how much would it cost those already living in the Central Borders? There was no answer to either query and the frustration of those citizens wishing to be involved, either for or against, was acute, as neither the essential information on which a choice could be made nor the machinery for putting the choice (if it was in favour of the Plan) into action were available.

D. Staffing and Management. It has long been appreciated that with a shortage of skilled manpower in Britain, local authorities have had particular difficulty in filling their posts, but there is a further problem in that those already employed show some restlessness. The Committee on the Staffing of Local Government found that 'about 48 per cent of men officers say they are seriously considering leaving local government or would consider doing so if it were not for loss of pension rights.' Many vacant posts are advertised repeatedly without producing suitable replies, some departments have been short of their approved establishments for years, while many of those employed do not have the necessary qualifications.

Recruitment of trainees and vacant and inadequately filled posts

Profession	Percentage of authorities experiencing 'extreme difficulty' in recruiting trainees	Percentage of vacant posts	Percentage of posts filled by staff with less than the desirable qualifications
Child Care Officers	47	7·2	43·6
Architects	38	17·4	13·3
Engineers – Civil and Municipal	33	8·8	13·9
Engineers – Structural	25	8·0	12·8
Weights and Measures Officers	25	4·1	1·3
Public Health Inspectors	24	11·4	3·8
Librarians	23	6·1	17·4
Accountants	21	2·7	27·8
Solicitors	21	4·4	1·2
Mental Health Workers	20	5·2	39·7
Planning Officers	20	8·3	17·8
Social Welfare Workers	20	3·1	40·3

It is clear that the recruitment of such categories as planners, architects, engineers and medical officers of health presents particular difficulties. The situation is also serious in some of the newer specialisms where the work is exacting and modern methods of training do make a great difference to the quality of service. Probably the best example is in child care.

Child Care Officers – Qualifications

Number in post	Profession-ally qualified	Holders of the Home Office Declaration of Recognition of Experience	Social science qualification only	No qualifica-tion
2,341	667 (28·4%)	210 (9%)	538 (23%)	926 (39·6%)

Residential Child Care Staff – Qualifications

Posts filled	Council's certificate in residential care	Related qualification in teaching, nursing, etc.	No qualification
5,035	526 (10·5%)	374 (7·5%)	4,135 (82%)

There are clearly some causes for this state of affairs that have nothing to do with the structure, standing and resources of local government. It is amazing, though typical of recent British government, that when a Committee was appointed under Sir George Mallaby to inquire into staffing, it operated entirely separately from the Committee on the Management of Local Government and both questions of salary scales and the structure of local government were excluded from its remit. It was asked only 'to consider the existing methods of recruiting local government officers and of using them; and what changes might help local authorities to get the best possible service and help their officers to give it'.

Yet certain conclusions could not help emerging. While the Committee's research gave 'no indication that the size of local authorities is in itself a significant factor in attracting recruits', they discovered 'that the larger counties and county boroughs are in a better position than the smaller ones in regard to planning staff', that 'counties with populations over 200,000 seem to be more successful in attracting qualified staff for their Treasurers' departments' and 'the largest county boroughs . . . have the fewest vacancies for valuers.' In each of the professional departments, it became clear that local authorities had to offer salaries comparable to those lawyers, doctors, planners and engineers could earn outside local government and that these salaries had to be related in turn to what the other officials, such as the Clerk to the Council, were paid. Thus it is not surprising that smaller counties or county boroughs or those with a low level of resources simply cannot afford enough to attract a full range of staff. Not only is there the problem of of salaries, but it is doubtful whether, to give one example, there is enough to do in all the 175 planning departments outside London to make the work appealing. Young and able entrants want an office of reasonable size with a constant flow of work and a proper career structure. In child care, for instance, there is a desire to specialize among newer entrants, while in the authorities with only a few cases a single officer has to cover all aspects of the department.

It is not difficult to agree with the cautious aside of the Committee on Staffing that if the Royal Commission on Local Government's 'recommendations result in the reduction of the number of local authorities and a consequent increase in the size of administrative units, it is our view that this will have a marked effect on the careers open to local government officers and possibly on the way officers are deployed'.

The deployment not only of officials but of elected members on councils through the committee system has become a major weakness and the system was rightly criticized by the Committee on the Management of Local Government under Sir John Maud, which reported in 1967. The practice of dividing council work into a series of departments each supervised and even actually administered by a committee of councillors dates from the last century, when the councils had little staff, few duties and preferred to do their own administration. It has continued partly because some statutes require a committee, partly because it is the expected form, and partly because the type of councillor coming forward likes to feel he is doing something he understands, which may be settling the colour of the tiles on the floor of the lavatory in a new primary school.

But the results are bad. An inordinate amount of time is taken (fifty-two hours a month) by the average councillor, the senior officials are not left to get on with their jobs, and issues of principle are lost in a welter of minutiae. Indeed in some cases the committees spend their time allocating individual houses or interviewing for the post of assistant school caretaker while a fairly determined senior official slowly but steadily establishes the broad policy in housing and education.

As there is no single leader, the mayor usually being absorbed by his ceremonial and 'above-the-battle' duties, and no 'cabinet', there is a lack of co-ordination in the work of many authorities. The councils seldom overrule the decisions of individual committees and the latter often pay more attention to the relevant central government department than to their place in any overall local policy or strategy. Nor is the co-ordination easy for the County or Town Clerk. Though it has often been suggested that the Clerk should be the chief officer of the authority, his position has remained ill-defined and in many cases the medical officer of health, the director of education and other principal officers do not accept that he is anything more than a first among equals. For all these reasons there is a tendency to fragmentation in local government work, the pace in each sector being determined by the personality of the senior officials, occasionally by the chairman of the committee, often by the dictates of the Whitehall Ministry. It is not surprising if the total effect of the system is to attract only the kind of member who finds the small matters actually left for local decision satisfying and to discourage those interested in policy and action. As the Committee on Management summed it up, 'there is often an absence of any real desire for change and a lack of awareness of the need for it. . . . Contentment with the present is perhaps the worst symptom of the ill health of local authorities'.

These then are the weaknesses of the present system: a poor electoral response, great difficulty in attracting suitable candidates, awkward, old-fashioned areas no longer in keeping with modern administrative problems, increased central government control, financial autonomy reduced to an almost negligible level and serious problems of staff shortage and internal structure. When considering the performance of local government, one is reminded of Dr Johnson's reaction in another context. It is 'like a dog's walking on his hinder legs. It is not done well; but you are surprised to find it done at all.'

Chapter 2
The Criteria of a Reformed System

It is typically British to imagine that it is possible to reform local government – or any other institution – without first being clear about its purpose, without first settling the value judgements and working out the objectives of the reformed institutions. It is assumed that by looking at the particular machinery, by taking evidence about how the present arrangements work, inconsistencies will emerge, obvious changes will suggest themselves and the problem will be solved.

Recent Governments have broken up the question of institutional reform into segments almost as if to ensure that the broader issues will not be discussed. At the moment of writing, some ministers, M.P.s and members of the public are considering methods of Parliamentary reform. Meanwhile, totally disconnected, the Fulton committee examined the personnel, professional structure and recruitment of the civil service. Both parliamentary and civil service reform closely affect local government but it is being reviewed in a totally separate compartment subdivided into three boxes labelled London (which has been 'done' by the Herbert Commission), England (the Maud Commission) and Scotland (the Wheatley Commission). There was a further sub-division, since staffing (in England only) was examined by a special Committee under Sir George Mallaby, and the management of local government was reviewed by a Committee under Sir John Maud, both of which reported in 1967. Yet for both staffing and management, a crucial question is the attitude of the civil service to regional and local administration. Is it better to give up the idea that central departments can only act through agencies such as *ad hoc* boards and local government? If Whitehall departments wish to control a policy, perhaps they should execute it themselves and leave local government the task of administering only those matters which can be totally entrusted to the local councils? On the other hand, if it is considered that the central government cannot handle the details of local investment programmes and if there is to be some real power given to re-formed local or regional government, this will have major repercussions in Whitehall. At present the departmental structure and loyalties are a major reason for the failures in regional government. The answer may have to be a new ministry or new structures in the existing ministries. Perhaps officials in the top-tier local authorities should be part of the central civil service or at least there should be periods of secondment from Whitehall. Similarly one of the factors inhibiting regional variations of central government policy is the present system of responsibility to the House of Commons. If it is wished to alter this and to give M.P.s some creative work or actual influence in their areas, it might be possible for M.P.s to sit on regional or top-tier local authority councils.

By subdividing the consideration of reform and failing to state the overall objectives clearly, many of these possibilities and interconnections were omitted. In addition, the terms of reference of the various committees and Royal Commissions were carefully limited so that there were areas of each of the separate aspects of the problems put before the committees which they were not allowed to consider. For instance, the Committee on Staffing were restricted to 'the *existing methods* of recruiting local government officers and of using them; and what changes might help local authorities to get the best possible service and help their officers to give it'. (My italics.)

That is to say the Committee were asked to work on the assumption that there would be no major reforms in the structure of local government (after all, these were being handled by another Commission) and they were not expected to consider alternative methods of recruitment even if the present structure was retained. Thus there was no examination of the virtues of a single local government service with a body which would recruit, fix the levels and grades of training and the pay for categories of posts while leaving the councils to select officers from this unified service for appointment to their staff. This system has been tried in countries overseas that have otherwise adopted the British pattern of local government. As has been said, there could be no consideration of how far it would be desirable to have civil servants from the central departments seconded for periods to local government and vice versa, nor could there be any examination of such questions as whether it was desirable, from the staff point of view, to keep the present tripartite structure of the Health Service. All that the Committee on Staffing could do in this last instance was to produce two stirring recommendations. The first was to local authorities to 'Note the changes which affect the recruitment and use of medical practitioners in the other two' (branches of the Health Service) and then to the Ministry of Health: 'The relative positions of medical practitioners in the local authority service and in the other two branches of the National Health Service should be re-examined.'

The Committee on Management had similarly restricted terms of reference, its task being 'to consider in the light of modern conditions how local government might best continue to attract and retain people (both elected representatives and principal officers) of the calibre necessary to ensure its maximum effectiveness'. This Committee, however, took a somewhat wider view of its task and examined local government procedure and internal organization abroad. It felt able to make a radical appraisal of the committee system, of departmental organization, of relations with the central government and the public, and conducted some research into the categories of persons elected to local councils. But again it was hampered by the need to start with the existing structure and system, so that there was no thorough consideration of the city manager or directly elected sole executive. Nor was there any examination of the problems that might arise in attracting suitable persons to serve on fewer larger councils, should there be a reform of structure. But within these limits, the Committee did produce a thorough and useful report.

The most striking and potentially serious restrictions were, however, imposed on the most important of the reviews, that undertaken by the two Royal Commissions on Local Government. They were told

to consider the structure of Local Government in England, outside greater London (or in Scotland), *in relation to its existing functions*; and to make recommendations for authorities and boundaries, and for functions and their division, having regard to the size and character of areas *in which these can be most effectively exercised* and the need to sustain a viable system of local democracy. (My italics.)

The first and greatest weakness of these terms of reference is that they limit the examination to the most suitable areas for the conduct of the *existing functions* of local government. Yet the present functions are not in any sense the pure essence of what local government ought to do; they are the entirely arbitrary collection of tasks left after some had been removed on the grounds that the existing units were too small, too poor or simply inappropriate. In this way over recent years local authorities have lost responsibility for main roads, some civil airfields, hospitals, public assistance, passenger road transport services, electricity supply and gas undertakings. It may be that these functions are better out of the hands of local authorities, but surely it was wrong to omit any consideration of whether larger units could resume them with general advantage.

Even more serious, the terms of reference prevented the Royal Commissions weighing the desirability of local government units big enough to take over the functions now given to the boards, bureaux and commissions of 'intermediate government'. A far better approach would have been to ask the Royal Commissions to consider not only the existing tasks of local government but to extend their survey to examine all functions which were conducted either by local government, by bodies outside the central departments or by central government itself, if these functions might usefully be devolved. The most obvious example is the work of the regional economic planning councils. Although these bodies are only advisory, if their plans include land use planning and are accepted, all the most important decisions about the local environment are settled. The more recent of these elaborate documents set out the location of new towns and roads, recommend which existing roads should be developed, earmark land for industrial estates, recreation and new housing, and suggest sites for technical colleges and the whole range of principal amenities. If the work is done properly and is endorsed by the local authorities and the central government, it pre-empts all the key lines of development. Refusal to consider this kind of planning, its progressive adaptation to circumstances and its implementation as proper functions for local government, might well take much of the meaning out of any reformed system.

The terms of reference do not mean that evidence on these issues was not presented to the Commissions or that they did not talk over this problem. The author gave evidence that included these questions, both in writing and orally, to the Scottish Royal Commission, and the D.E.A. also mentioned regional planning in its evidence to the English Royal Commission. But the terms of reference do require the Commissions to ignore any arguments relating to the performance of functions other than the existing functions of local government in coming to their conclusions. Because most of the functions that require large regional units have already been taken away from local government or, if they are new functions, were never awarded to local government, this has effectively removed all the strongest arguments for really large units from the purview of the Commissions. In effect it would be possible to propose a reformed system for conducting the existing activities of local government, and central government might (it is at least theoretically possible!) be reformed both in Westminster and in Whitehall, and yet one of the major weaknesses of the present system would remain in the form of regional or national boards, advisory committees, development commissions, planning councils and so on, all performing important duties yet untouched by these reforms and outside the effective democratic control either of M.P.s or of local government councillors.

The question of democratic control occurs in the last line of the terms of reference: 'the need to sustain a viable system of local democracy'. It is not clear what 'viable' means in this context but evidently a factor to be taken into consideration is whether any new structure of local government can attract and hold public interest, and excite participation more effectively than the present range of councils. Yet there is considerable evidence that while the public are not very interested in the circumscribed functions at present performed by local government, they are much more ready to take an active part in the strategic decisions affecting the life of a locality which are not at present entrusted to local government. The best example again is the regional planning councils. When these began it was thought that they presented an opportunity for shaping a whole locality or region from the point of view of those resident in the area. The result was a great clamour for appointment and precisely the sort of leading professional, industrial and trade union personalities were coming forward whose absence from the existing councils is so much lamented. Yet if these functions cannot be considered by the Royal Commissions as suitable for local government, then electors and potential councillors cannot be blamed if they show little interest.

This aspect is particularly evident in the cases of Wales and of Scotland where one form of reformed local government would be a single unit assembly or council for the whole country. There are arguments based on function (to be examined later) which would point to three regions in Wales and to six or seven regional divisions in Scotland, but there are also arguments which would point to a single unit in each case. It would be a pity if the latter arguments were discounted merely because they depend in part on the importance of transferring functions which do not at present lie with local government. Whatever is thought of the merits of the case for total independence in Scotland and Wales, the rise of the nationalist parties has shown that there is far more interest in such nation-wide decisions and therefore in a single unit government, than in a series of internal regions: the former is far more democratically viable and it would be a great mistake if the Royal Commission on Local Government in Scotland were not able to take this into account. There is no Royal Commission on Welsh Local Government but any decision on its future would be profoundly affected by a recommendation that the top-tier unit of elected local government in Scotland should cover the whole country.

The Criteria to be used here

This book is not the place for an examination of the more abstract arguments for or against democracy but it must be recognized that these arguments underlie many of the attitudes to local government reform. There are two basic schools of thought. The first was cited by the Committee on Management when it said that 'Parliament, Ministers and the Whitehall departments have come increasingly to lose faith in the responsibility of locally elected bodies'. The withdrawal of tasks from local government, preference for appointed boards and increased control over functions and finance, have all been the deliberate product of this distaste for local democracy. While M.P.s and Ministers would shy away from any admission that they disliked such an 'all right' concept as local democracy, in practice many would applaud a Labour Minister forcing a policy of comprehensive schools on one group of authorities or a Conservative Minister using his reserve powers to force others to review their council house rents. Local democracy, by all means, but not if this allows a local council, resting on the wishes of its own electors, to go its own way.

There are two very strong strains in contemporary British government, the power of the executive to get what it wants and the power of the central departments of state to impose a single pattern on the whole country, both of which must be offended and indeed seriously curtailed if local democracy is to exist in any meaningful way. It would be unrealistic to ignore the fact that to produce a democratic and effective series of local councils would mean stemming the tide of centralization, uniformity, and suspicion of popular, elected government that has been flowing with increasing force for twenty years. Therefore it will be bitterly resisted by many in both major parties, in the civil service, in industry and among the pressure groups used to operating on a nation-wide but London-centred basis.

So the concept of democracy adopted here is the assumption that there should be machinery for separating the important decisions from the mass of routine issues and that all such decisions should be taken by an executive which can be held electorally responsible and should be subjected to scrutiny, discussion and endorsement by an elected assembly. Some of these decisions will be on matters that affect the whole nation in the same way; these are therefore better settled by the central government. But there are others where it is possible and desirable that sections of the community might wish to act in a special way or to place a different interpretation on the matter. Democratic local government should be organized on one or more levels so that all questions where variations in different parts of the country are possible and desirable should be under local control, while the rest are watched over by Parliament with no room for matters to slip between these two forms of democratic supervision. It may be thought that this evades part of the problem because there will be differences about how much local variation is desirable. To go back to the earlier example, many educational reformers would argue that if comprehensive education is the best, then it should be enforced on the whole country or if economic rents are a step towards solving the housing problem, then no local authority should be able to stand in the way of this policy.

But education and housing are matters where local or regional policies need not have adverse effects on the nation as a whole; in these decisions value judgements are involved where no one is entitled to claim that he knows best what is good for other people and there is plenty of evidence that these are precisely the sort of issues that Londoners, the Scots, Yorkshiremen or the citizens of Bristol wish to settle for themselves.

With, then, this definition of 'a viable local democracy', it is also evident that the various functions that ought to be settled outside Whitehall each have different optimum areas in terms of population, resources or geography. Wanting good services, the public will not wish child care given to units where there are not enough children to merit a proper staff nor can river pollution be managed by an authority which does not include most of the river in question. It would be possible in theory to construct an administrative or local government unit for each service. At one time in the nineteenth century when democracy was on the ascendant there were attempts on these lines with separate elections to police, lighting and paving, and education authorities. Similarly, now that democracy is in decline, there has been a tendency to create *ad hoc* nominated bodies for hospitals, planning and public utilities, each with its own most suitable area of coverage. But the public could not contemplate such a multiplicity of elections nor could candidates be found for so many single-purpose authorities. A solution has to be found by selecting areas which suit the largest number and most important local functions and which coincide with local sentiment, so that a feeling of loyalty to the community can be used to create and maintain popular interest.

In the case of civic sentiments, people have loyalties at several levels – to the town, island or valley where they live, in some cases to a larger area as Londoners, Geordies or Welshmen, and then to Britain as a whole. These sentiments must be matched with the optimum areas for local government services, the latter being considered in terms of resources and capacity to attract suitable staff and population, the object being to produce a simple system of tiers of self-government, stretching from the immediate locality to the national level.

It is hard to be precise about local sentiments, especially when there is a tendency for such feelings only to focus round existing administrative units. Nevertheless, some observations can be made with reasonable confidence. There is a pride in Londoners and also a sense of attachment to some, particularly the older, boroughs. London government has capitalized on these feelings in probably the most effective way possible. Outside London, there is the usual loyalty to the older towns and cities but regional feelings seem to grow stronger the farther away from London, there being more of a sense of identity in the South-West, in Yorkshire and Lancashire than in, say, the east Midlands, while in Wales and Scotland there are quasi-national traditions to produce an even stronger sense of identity than in Cornwall or Northumberland.

A list of functions which are or could be undertaken by local authorities would include:

Functions	Most Appropriate Unit (or the present number of units where these are suitable)
1. Devising of regional economic plans, collection of statistics	8 Regions in England plus Scotland and Wales.
2. Generation and supply of electricity	14 Electricity Boards.
3. Manufacture and supply of gas	12 Area Gas Boards.
4. Construction and maintenance of motorways, highways, trunk roads, ferries and road safety	Large regional units.
5. Supervision of and advice about agriculture and fisheries	Large regional units.
6. Universities, Teacher Training colleges and central educational institutions	Large regional units.
7. Forestry	Large regional units.
8. Prison Service	Large regional units.
9. Valuation	Large regional units.
10. Registration of Births, Marriages and Deaths	Large regional units.
11. Probation Services	Large regional units.
12. Remand Homes	Large regional units
13. Police	National force to several regional forces.
14. Execution of local economic development schemes	Size of conurbations or special problem areas.
15. Town and country planning	11 regions including Scotland and Wales.

Functions	Most Appropriate Unit (or the present number of units where these are suitable)
16. Hospital Services	13 regions in England.
17. Airports	Large regional units.
18. River purification and flood prevention	River catchment areas. 200,000 upwards
19. Principal roads	50 units about 1 million on average.
20. Youth Employment Service	300,000 upwards (Ministry of Labour)
21. Water supply and sewage disposal	250,000 (Ministry of Housing).
22. Fire	50 units about 1 million on average.
23. Education	300,000–500,000 (Ministry of Education).
24. Child care	250,000 upwards (Home Office).
25. Food and milk administration	200,000 upwards.
26. Libraries and Museums	100,000 upwards (Ministry of Housing).
27. Local Health and Welfare Services	200,000 upwards (Ministry of Health).
28. Food and drugs regulations, weights and measures	60,000 upwards (Ministry of Housing).
29. Allotments	
30. Burial and Cremation	
31. Clean Air	
32. Coast Protection	
33. Entertainments	
34. Housing (in addition to regional powers)	All suitable for minor authorities of about 40,000 people upwards.
35. Physical Training and Recreation	
36. Public Parks	
37. Public Ways and Footpaths	
38. Refuse collection	
39. Slaughterhouses	
40. Taxicab licensing	
41. Classified and other roads	

With this variety of optimum areas for functions and the type of local loyalty or sentiment already described, only a limited number of solutions are possible. All involve a two- or three-tier system in order to group functions in units which would be appropriate to democratic control, but while a variety of second-tier unit sizes are possible, it is clear that there are two major alternative types of solution to the problem of the top-tier unit. The first is to create thirty to forty city regions of 250,000 to over a million which would allow all functions from 9 downwards to be allocated to local government. (Though larger regions would possibly be better for functions 9 to 12, they could nevertheless be entrusted to such authorities.) The second solution would be to have ten to fifteen large regional units (counting Scotland and Wales each as a single unit) which would permit all these functions to be transferred to local government, thus producing a genuine element of devolution. In both cases functions 29 to 41 could well be performed by the second-tier local government units, but the precise level of allocation between first- and second-tier units would depend on the size of the top-tier units and on whether the smaller units would all be of roughly the same size or would fluctuate with local demographic conditions and thus perhaps permit a different degree of delegation.

There are a number of hybrid solutions possible such as city regions for the conurbations with amalgamated counties in the rest of the country. For political reasons the Government might decide on large provincial regions in England but deliberately divide Scotland and Wales into smaller units; that is if there is a desire to resist rather than utilize the positive aspects of nationalism. Also the structure may appear somewhat different depending on which tier is given the most importance. As the broader functions of economic and land use planning, of transport and urban redevelopment are the most important, it might seem natural to place the emphasis on the top tier. But if the central government is frightened of a vigorous local democracy, if it wishes to retain the salient local decisions in its own hands, it may place most emphasis (as in the G.L.C. area) on the second-tier units, making them larger and stronger. Then it would be possible to have a large regional upper tier operating more on an advisory or co-ordinating basis alongside the regional arms of the central departments and manned not by direct elections but by delegates from the elected second-tier authorities.

Even if any of these hybrid solutions are recommended by the Royal Commission, the basic arguments still centre on the dispute between the city region and the provincial region as the most appropriate top-tier unit. Therefore the next three chapters examine these two solutions, in order to set out the main alternatives open to the Government.

Chapter 3
The City Region
Solution

Of the two major choices before the Royal Commission, this at one time seemed to be the most likely, though there could have been minor additions or variations such as representation of the city regions on larger, purely advisory bodies similar to the present Planning Councils. There are three reasons why this school of thought was strongly represented on the Royal Commission. The first is that the Commission was appointed on the advice of Mr R. H. S. Crossman, then the Minister for Housing and Local Government. As the M.P. for Coventry East, he was impressed by the vigour of the City Council and by the arguments that larger units need go no further than the type of region of which Coventry might well be the centre. As he told the Town Planning Institute in 1965, he envisaged a reform which would produce single upper-tier authorities 'the area of Coventry, Rugby and the countryside up to the Birmingham green belt', and his appointments to the Royal Commission tended to reflect his views. It is possible that later, when his responsive mind grasped the significance of Scottish and Welsh nationalism and when he realized the difficulties the regional planning councils were encountering, he might have wanted to unpack the Royal Commission and repack it with those who were more impressed with the case for larger regional units, but by then the Commission had started work.

The second reason is the terms of reference of the Royal Commission. As has been explained, these terms did not preclude arguments in favour of the larger regions or provinces as some have called them. N.A.L.G.O., the Liberal Party, the Town and Country Planning Association, the Architect's Association, the Local Government Study Group of Manchester University and the Society of Town Clerks all gave evidence in favour of large regions. But the terms of reference did mean that the Commission's attention was concentrated on the best way of performing *the existing functions* of local government. As a result arguments in favour of more devolution and of the assumption by local government of powers given to other regional bodies were heard but not fully deployed.

The final reason is that Whitehall has plumped for this solution. Realizing that local government had to be revived and that democratic forms would have to be retained, the major departments of state concentrated simply on seeking the most efficient units to perform what is now left to the existing authorities, and clearly wanted no truck with any solution which would permit either a wider degree of local autonomy or actual transfer of functions from Whitehall to local government. There are sometimes complaints about politicians following a party line but seldom has there been such unanimity as when ministry followed ministry, whether it was Education wanting an optimum population of 500,000 or Local Government suggesting 100,000 as the best number for a library service, in concluding (often with little or no evidence) that thirty to forty upper-tier units would provide the answer. Only the Treasury, the Ministry of Labour and the Ministry of Agriculture, Fisheries and Food failed to mention these precise figures, but the weight of their evidence went in the same direction.

As for the arguments for the city region solution, they were most cogently set out by Mr Derek Senior (who was appointed by Mr Crossman to the Commission) in an article in Volume 36 of the *Political Quarterly* (Jan.–March 1965), aspects of the case being commented on by Professor J. A. G. Griffith in *New Society* on 21 October 1965 and by Michael Steed in the same periodical on 28 December 1967.

The case rests on the assumption that it is the task of the central government to work out economic strategy at the regional level. Mr Senior held that

planning can make no headway unless central government does organize itself to think with one mind about all aspects of physical development and takes the initiative in formulating regional *strategies*, on whatever scale it finds convenient for the timing and relative location of major resources, industrial, commercial and recreational developments and of the communications between them.

Once having posited that this has to be done by outlying branches of the central government, Mr Senior argues that agencies must exist to translate such strategies into land use plans and to carry out the plans. To do this properly larger units than the present local authorities are needed (but clearly smaller than the economic planning regions). Because the major land use problems are housing, location of industry, travel to work, and siting of amenities, the answer is to select as local government units geographical areas in which these authorities have a focal point. Boundaries should be drawn at the watershed where family A tumbles into its car to go to shop, work, school, or a concert and drives east, while family B further down the road prefers, for the same facilities, to drive west. According to this argument people look for many services to the nearest large urban centre, and so the best units for providing these services, for carrying out strategic economic plans and for rallying a sense of local involvement and loyalty are city regions. Looking at the actual position, Mr Senior distinguishes four kinds of city regions in England, the mature, the emergent, the embryonic and the potential.

The 'mature' are those where some two million people

already have access to and the habit of relying on a single near-by major city, usually within an hour's drive, and apart from London the list consists of Birmingham, Manchester, Liverpool, Leeds and Newcastle. Had the discussion included Scotland, no doubt Glasgow would have been added to this group. The 'emergent' cities are Nottingham, Sheffield, Preston (with reservations), Southampton, Cardiff and Bristol, as they have 'ample dependent populations (over one million each), but their centres are as yet either not so readily accessible from some parts of their hinterlands or for various reasons less fully equipped'. In Scotland, Edinburgh would probably fall into this category. Then the 'embryonic' city regions are Swansea, Brighton, Hull, Leicester, Norwich, Stoke-on-Trent, Oxford, Exeter, Cambridge, Coventry, Middlesborough and Gloucester (Aberdeen and Dundee), all with hinterlands of between 300,000 and 800,000 people. Finally, the 'potential' group includes a ring of towns to be developed around London – Ashford, Newbury, Northampton, Ipswich, Peterborough and Bournemouth – while the remaining areas would have to be grouped around Carlisle, Shrewsbury (linked to a new town in mid-Wales), Plymouth, Lincoln, York, Bangor and presumably Ayr and Inverness, though in some cases the total population drops to a little under 300,000.

The claim being made is not that the last two groups exist as social units grouped around a city at the moment, but 'that the city region, even in its embryonic form, is a social entity much more relevant to the concerns of local government than any other now that the motor vehicle has come into general use'. With minimum populations of around 250,000, even the weakest of such authorities could manage functions 13 to 41 listed on pages 49–50. Mr Senior believes they

would be ideally equipped in catchment area, caseload and financial resources to be responsible for the management of a unified, positive health service (including health centres and

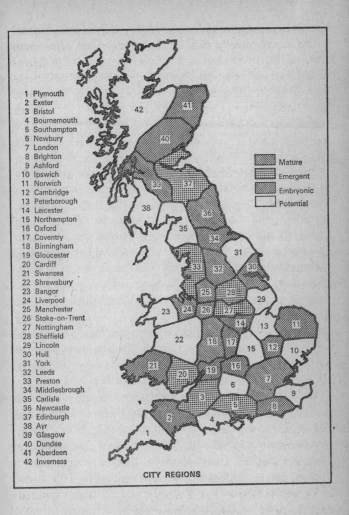

1 Plymouth
2 Exeter
3 Bristol
4 Bournemouth
5 Southampton
6 Newbury
7 London
8 Brighton
9 Ashford
10 Ipswich
11 Norwich
12 Cambridge
13 Peterborough
14 Leicester
15 Northampton
16 Oxford
17 Coventry
18 Birmingham
19 Gloucester
20 Cardiff
21 Swansea
22 Shrewsbury
23 Bangor
24 Liverpool
25 Manchester
26 Stoke-on-Trent
27 Nottingham
28 Sheffield
29 Lincoln
30 Hull
31 York
32 Leeds
33 Preston
34 Middlesbrough
35 Carlisle
36 Newcastle
37 Edinburgh
38 Ayr
39 Glasgow
40 Dundee
41 Aberdeen
42 Inverness

Mature
Emergent
Embryonic
Potential

CITY REGIONS

hospitals), of traffic, commuter transport and regional motorways, of seaports and airports, land drainage and water supply,
for all higher education short of university standard, for
organizing the demand for house-building components . . .
for the comprehensive renewal of city centres, for the abatement
of air and river pollution and the reclamation of derelict land,
for crime squads and multi-purpose sports centres, for the promotion of regional development and for the making of development plans.

Clearly this proposal has its attractions. In one sense it ends
the division between town and countryside and provides
authorities large enough for all existing local government
activities with the possibility of handing over some, such as
hospitals and river pollution, that are at present left with *ad
hoc* bodies. In practical terms such a solution has some chance
of acceptance in that, while many in the present councils will
be unhappy, the forty-two cities named will presumably be
willing to give their support, while Whitehall clearly prefers
this to any of the alternatives.

In political terms there can be few objections. Till the land-
slide of the 1968 local elections, the Conservatives have held
nine of these cities since 1945 and Labour twelve. There is the
added political attraction for some members of both major
parties that this solution cuts right across the arguments of the
nationalists. It does so by implying that there is a more genuine
sense of community in the Highlands, the Clyde Valley or the
North-East than in Scotland as a whole and that north, south
and mid Wales all have more in common with the neighbouring areas of England than with each other. This is prac-
tically demonstrated in that the Carlisle city region spans the
Solway and thus the English-Scottish border, while Liverpool
includes Flint and parts of Denbigh and the Shrewsbury city
region is so drawn as to include Montgomery, Radnor and
sections of Merioneth and Cardigan.

Disadvantages of City Regions

The first weakness of this proposal is that at the moment its thesis, that all of Britain looks to one or other of forty-two cities, simply is not true and would therefore produce gross distortion if it was made the basis of a system of local government. While the argument may hold for areas around Birmingham, Leeds or Glasgow, some parts of the country are only fitted in by taking a vacant area and searching for a moderate-sized town in it. The system is at its weakest in the rural parts of Britain where there is not the same orientation towards city life and its attractions and there may be no single acceptable focal point. Thus all Cornwall does not look to Plymouth, North Wales to Bangor or the seven Highland counties to Inverness. It is also inappropriate in the areas near major conurbations where there are a number of moderate-sized towns but no city acting as a centre. This is particularly true in the neighbourhood of London where it is hard to imagine what Newbury or Ashford can offer that is not better provided either by the local shopping centre or by a trip into London. The same is true of the Midlands and the North, one example being that Preston certainly is not and probably never will be regarded as a centre providing services to an area stretching from Blackpool on the one side to Blackburn on the other.

This leads to one of the deeper weaknesses of the scheme: while it ends the old distinction between town and country, it introduces the new and rather invidious notion that all proper local organizations and activity should be city-based. The assumption is that without a centre point in a city, proper amenities and a high standard in certain services cannot be provided. There are two objections to this. The first is that local government may be more concerned with solving other kinds of problems. For instance, the reason why there is a case for treating central Wales or the Highlands or the South West as a unit is not because each centres on a city (they do not) but because each of these areas has special needs which are better tackled by a single administration. The second is that while the original effect of widespread car ownership may have been to allow people to dash into the nearest town, this has now caused the most severe traffic congestion and social distortions. A major objective of regional planners is to have an adequate transport system so that in a large local government area, covering a number of towns, one can be used as the cultural centre, one contains the industrial training facilities, while a third may be developed as a centre for recreational amenities. Indeed, it may often make good sense to have the administrative headquarters of a region outside the most congested of the existing urban centres.

All this suggests that there are other considerations which may be more useful or more relevant in selecting the future local government units than the undoubted convenience of simply enlarging the scope of some of our bigger cities. Of these other considerations, the strongest in administrative terms is that the city region cannot, as its proponents have in fact conceded, take on some of the major functions at present entrusted to larger regional authorities or regional offices of the central departments. Of these, by far the most important is regional economic and land use planning. Here it is agreed that units roughly of the size of the planning regions created in 1965 by George Brown (each roughly a tenth of the country) are required, yet Senior assumes that the tasks of these 'little Whitehalls' could never be transferred to local government Professor J. A. G. Griffith has said 'no one claims that, had local authorities been fewer and larger, they would have been entrusted with the functions of these councils, still less with the functions of these boards'.

But this has been suggested and is being put forward now. For if the regional councils have their advice taken, this would determine most of the key decisions in the local government sphere – siting of industry, new housing estates, major roads, amenity centres and so on. To go down to city regions for a first-tier local authority either means that a nominated or delegated intermediate tier will have to remain or that the central departments will have to abandon their regional structure and take more decisions in Whitehall. Either result would be contrary to two of the objectives set out in the previous chapter: to devolve more powers from central to local government and to remove the need for an intermediate tier of nominated authorities.

Also the city regions would, in many cases, be too lacking in population and resources to have such tasks as the generation and supply of electricity and of gas, the construction of highways and the handling of higher education restored or given to them. It is also doubtful whether the weaker of the city regions could undertake all the functions ascribed to them by Senior. For instance, there are fourteen hospital boards at present in England and it is very doubtful whether it would be advisable to divide their tasks among thirty-two city regions. Similarly, control of river pollution and water supply would only be possible if joint authorities were created. The problems of traffic in south Lancashire would be divided between three city regions, and the system assumes that in the southern part of the county everyone wants a pattern of communications running either into Liverpool or Manchester. This is simply not the case and would produce serious distortions and hardships in some of the smaller towns. Other functions would still remain matters for negotiation between authorities, Glasgow having to settle its overspill programme with the other Scottish city regions while London would be exporting people to the string of surrounding minor city regions. This division would retain the problem of many people living in one local government area and commuting to work in another. It is doubtful whether thirty-two fire services in England is the best arrangement and this number of police forces is almost certainly undesirable. Even in terms of present local government functions such as education and child care, some of these regions would be at the lowest level in terms of population and resources. It may be said that it is unfair to pick on the weakest and poorest of the potential city regions but experience has shown that a system of local government is as strong as its weakest link and that the degree of central government control and supervision will be devised not to suit the capacities of Leeds or Liverpool but of Ashford or Ayr.

There is also a special problem about second-tier units in city regions. It is generally agreed that a smaller unit would be needed but how would the main city be handled within a city region? If Birmingham, for instance, was treated as a single second-tier unit, it might well dominate the city region and have an absolute majority of elected members on the regional council. In any case, outlying boroughs that had lost their status during the change over to city regions would be quick to suspect and resent any hint of such a situation. The alternatives would be either to have no second tier in the main city or to cut the city up into wards. If the main city had to rely on the regional council and its administration while the surrounding areas were partially run by second-tier councils, there would be constant accusations that the city was getting preference, that the regional officials worked there and gave it the lion's share of their time. On the other hand, it might be argued that the larger cities could be divided into smaller boroughs but while the London boroughs have some separate character and identity, it would be ludicrous and most unpopular to try and cut up Birmingham or Newcastle and pretend that thereafter the city from which the region took its name did not exist as an administrative unit.

In terms of the popular enthusiasm or sentiment which elected units must build up if they are to survive, there is little case for the city regions. As has been said, to set them up in a fashion which appeared to challenge the concept of Scottish and Welsh identity (a more moderate and widespread feeling than that of extreme political nationalism) and which crossed the old frontiers would be bitterly resented. Similarly in England, there is pride in coming from the South-West or in being a Londoner or a Geordie and there is civic pride in the cities but it is doubtful whether small towns and the surrounding rural areas which have clung to their own identity could ever work up any enthusiasm for the proposed city regions. While Scottish and Welsh patriotism exists beyond a doubt, a case can be made out that there is more reality in regional feeling than in any loyalty to forty-two selected cities. There is pride in being a Highlander, a Scotsman and, for many, in being British, but to ask those living in Harris or Orkney to feel an attachment to the Inverness city region would be a risky venture. Similarly people who come from the South-West are proud of the fact, but to call for loyalty to the Plymouth city region would receive rude rejoinders from some local inhabitants; and many living in East Anglia feel attached to neither Ipswich nor Norwich.

It is understandable that those who have battled so long and so fruitlessly for local government reform and who have felt the deep suspicion of any real counterpart to central government, may grasp at the city region as the best they can hope for. Yet this coming reform of local government (and one trusts something must happen, there must be some changes after the Royal Commission has reported) may well be the last major re-organization this century. If it is to last, it must take note of the increasing popular desire for participation, the desire to be informed and to be consulted, and if these desires are to be met, the reform must be far-reaching and have a real impact on the public. All decisions, local or national, must be made after proper questioning, debate and discussion by a popular assembly. It would be tragic if, after all this thought and effort, there was still a series of nominated bodies meeting in private, receiving secret information, taking vital decisions behind closed doors where neither M.P.s, local councillors, nor through them the public, are able to find out what is happening, all because the top tier of local government was still, despite the reforms, not strong enough to do its job.

Chapter 4
The Conurbation
and Enlarged County
Solution

Before considering the principal alternative to the 30–40 city region model, that is the 10 – 15 large regions or provinces, it is worth considering one hybrid solution, an adaptation of the city region proposal to the facts of the distribution of population and to political pressures. One weakness, as has been argued, of the city region concept is that it simply does not fit the existing pattern of urban development. In this case, it would be relatively easy to accept the seven 'mature' city regions or conurbations as units. There would be little political difficulty as each (London, Glasgow, Birmingham, Manchester, Liverpool, Leeds and Newcastle) is already the centre for a powerful local authority. The boundaries could be handled as they were in the case of London by extending as far as the limit of the built-up area or up to the edge of what might be regarded as the countryside. There would be difficulties with some neighbouring towns which have a strong sense of identity: should the Newcastle conurbation include Sunderland, Manchester include Bolton, Leeds include Bradford, Birmingham incorporate Wolverhampton, and so on? However, assuming that these could be resolved and conurbation boundaries fixed, the next step would be to group existing counties, cutting the forty-five English counties to some twenty-one in number and reducing Wales from thirteen counties to the five suggested in the 1967 White Paper on Local Government in Wales (Cmnd. 3340).

The result would be a total of six conurbations and some

twenty-six counties in England and Wales as top-tier authorities. A guide to the possible size and rateable value of these units is given in this table:

Conurbations

	Population	Rateable Value (£ million)
London	7,913,600	646
Birmingham	1,899,950	86·3
Leeds	1,145,370	42·2
Liverpool	1,144,240	16·9
Manchester	1,483,009	57·9
Newcastle	754,190	29

Enlarged Counties in England

	Population	Rateable Value (£ million)
Cornwall and Devon	876,500	38·0
Somerset and Dorset	885,114	34
Wiltshire and Gloucestershire	1,007,227	36·3
Berks, Hants and Isle of Wight	1,462,280	62·2
East Sussex and Kent	1,707,000	73·2
West Sussex and Surrey	1,377,500	77·8
Norfolk and E. and W. Suffolk	812,960	24·3
Beds, Huntingdon and Cambs	753,130	31·9
Hertfordshire and Essex	1,949,780	99·7
Bucks and Oxfordshire	781,280	39·4
Leicestershire, Northants and Rutland	767,010	29·2
Lincolnshire (all parts)	611,666	23·2
Notts and Derbyshire	1,394,233	47·3
Hereford, Salop and Worcs	·885,080	32
Warwickshire and Staffs	1,235,200	45·1
Lancashire	2,366,020	80·9
Cheshire	1,023,860	42·7
West Riding	1,734,576	48·7
East and North Riding	673,790	24·3
Cumberland and Westmorland	292,260	9·7
Northumberland and Durham	1,432,673	45·3

Enlarged Counties in Wales

	Population	Rateable Value (£ million)
Gwynedd	553,460	18·6
Powys	116,470	2·7
Dyfed	316,640	8·8
Gwent	419,990	12·1
Glamorgan	721,820	22·3

Not only would such a solution be relatively easy in the conurbations, but it would arouse the minimum resistance in the counties. Politically, the Labour–Conservative balance would, in normal years, tend to continue at roughly its present position. This approach was foreshadowed in the instructions given to the Local Government Commission set up in 1958, as it was empowered to look in particular at certain special review areas, Tyneside, West Yorkshire, South-East Lancashire, Merseyside and the West Midlands which were, in fact, the conurbations apart from London. The results of this method of tackling the problem can be seen in the G.L.C. and in the Local Government Commission's proposals for Tyneside and for Greater Manchester (and in the earlier work of the Local Government Boundary Commission). In such a reformed pattern, the second tier could also follow traditional divisions in that the boroughs amalgamated into conurbations could remain on the lines of the London boroughs and the enlarged counties could be divided into county borough and larger rural district councils.

Units of the size listed above could undertake all current local authority functions and the division between first- and second-tier functions could remain more or less as at present. The average size of both top- and second-tier units would be considerably larger, but this is desirable in that all the functions being performed by local government could be better managed if the units were larger.

Thus this solution has many attractions but it also has even more serious defects than the city region proposal. That had the merit of overcoming the town–countryside distinction which has done so much damage to any sensible organization of services. This suggestion would perpetuate this defect in that the conurbations would be cut off from the surrounding countryside and the existing borough–county division would be maintained at second-tier level in the enlarged counties. Probably the conurbations would, like Greater London, claim and receive more powers than could be given to the counties. There would then be the same battles at recurrent intervals as Sheffield or Edinburgh claimed conurbation status while the enlarged counties round about and the boroughs close to the cities resisted the proposal.

More serious, it would be impossible to allocate such areas regional planning powers so that a nominated tier of regional authorities would still be required between local and central government. Even minor planning functions could scarcely be delegated since the counties and conurbations would have to be supervised to ensure that main roads, for instance, running out from the built-up area into the surrounding countryside were properly sited. (This has happened in the case of the G.L.C. where trunk roads have remained the responsibility of the Ministry of Transport while metropolitan roads fall to the G.L.C. and side roads to the boroughs.) In addition to main roads, these top-tier units could not handle the supervision of amenity areas, preservation of the countryside, river pollution, main water supplies, they could not provide hospital services and thus run a unified health service, city airports might be outside the boundaries of conurbation, nor could the latter cope with their own overspill problems. The majority of the *ad hoc* bodies which cause so much confusion and slow down administration would remain, there could be no devolution of central government powers, no local authority protection of consumer interests on gas, electricity or transport boards. In short, this scheme would simply buy time by increasing the size of present local government units, thus removing only one defect of the existing system while preserving all the others.

Chapter 5
The Provincial or Large Regional Unit Solution

The origins of this method of solving the problem are complex. For all sorts of reasons, bodies faced with the necessity or desirability of operating from more than one centre have chosen to work in a number of regions. The conurbation or city region idea naturally came more readily to thoughtful members of existing city administrations who wanted to draw in the commuter and holiday hinterland. But those working at the national level who wish to subdivide have had no reason for choosing such an urban-oriented scheme. Thus government departments wanting closer contacts with outlying areas divided Britain into regions, appointing regional controllers. Large-scale industry, hoping to avoid a top-heavy administration, devised regions which fitted their production or marketing patterns, whichever were the more important. For economists, considering the persistence of different wage-levels and degrees of unemployment in different parts of the country, it has become normal to talk in terms of regions, and policies have been devised specifically in order to restore a proper balance of economic advantage between the regions. Geographers, planners and particularly those concerned with transport and urban renewal have also thought in these terms. Scotsmen indignantly reject the notion of 'being a region' and there is no implication here that either Scotland or Wales lack special features which entitle them to claim a difference of kind. But it remains true that Scotland, and to some extent Wales, have been administered by departments which have responsibilities for an area, or a region, rather than for a particular subject or service, as is the pattern in the U.K.

It is, therefore, not surprising that those wishing to reform local government and looking for units which would both offer a sound basis for administration and permit an element of devolution, have turned to the idea of large-scale regions as the top tier in a new system of local government. One immediate problem is that since this interest in regionalism has come from so many sources and for so many reasons, a wide variety of regions have been designated. For instance, by the Second World War it had been accepted that regional organization was helpful in co-ordinating and energizing services if there was an emergency. (The reason why regional organization was only thought to be of use in such circumstances was that it might violate the concept of ministerial responsibility. If, for instance, the Ministry of Agriculture's regional controllers adopted slightly different methods in different parts of the country, it would become evident that these actions were not all those of the Minister, and that officials had actually taken decisions on policy questions.) Thus, in 1939, England was divided into nine Civil Defence Regions, each with a regional 'capital' and a commissioner who was empowered to co-ordinate the work of local authorities in civil defence matters. The other major departments appointed officials on the same regional basis, partly to co-ordinate with civil defence, partly because the full utilization of scarce resources required a regional approach, partly to administer food controls and rationing. This elaborate system was never fully utilized because a full-scale emergency never arose and there were mixed opinions as to how well the function of co-ordination and elimination of regional bottlenecks was performed. While the office of commissioner was abolished in 1945, post-war reconstruction required much the same kind of flexible machinery and in 1946 the Treasury tried to achieve a measure of stand-ardization. A fixed set of regions was defined (see map on page 73) and other departments were asked to fit into the same boundaries so that co-operation between regional officials would be made easier. Nearly all departments did so, strength-ening their regional apparatus, and this machinery was used to further the distribution of industry, the housing drive and the first attempt at a government-controlled land use policy. After 1951, when the Conservatives dismantled much of the interventionist machinery of the war and post-war period, regional offices were cut down in numbers or closed. But there was a more fundamental problem than the change in the politi-cal and economic atmosphere. Regional officers with real powers to take decisions, alter priorities and perhaps thus incur more expenditure, did not fit into the Whitehall departmental system; their existence was a threat to Treasury control and to the convention of ministerial responsibility. With interest in regional administration waning, the Treasury after 1956 ceased to insist on departments obtaining its sanction if they wished to depart from the Standard Region boundaries in any devolu-tion of tasks outside Whitehall.

Nevertheless, the Standard Treasury Regions have remained as one of the patterns often adopted by those who advocate a few large top-tier local government units. These regions were devised chiefly as the pattern which would require least adap-tation if all the departments were to fall into line. They were not based on the primacy of any one function and so the boun-daries have some disadvantages for many of the tasks which such units would have to perform. For instance, accepting that economic and land use planning, urban renewal and commuter transport are key functions either for devolved central govern-ment or for top-tier local government, there are obvious anomalies in some of the boundaries. Probably the most serious is the division of London between three regions. The

THE NINE STANDARD TREASURY REGIONS

East Anglia thus produced contains large sections of outer London and combines them in an area including Norfolk and the Isle of Ely whose interests have little connection with those of southern Essex or Hertfordshire. Another deficiency is the straggling shape of the South Central Region which includes Dorset, in many ways part of the South-West, together with Oxfordshire and Buckinghamshire which, if anything, look to London. By having the northern boundary of the East Midlands Region running along the Humber, that estuary is divided when both shores should clearly be administered as a single unit. At the same time, putting the whole of the North Riding into the North-East is a mistake and unduly restricts the scope of the Yorkshire Region. The Standard Treasury Regions accepted the treatment of Scotland and Wales as single units; the only serious difficulty which this created in terms of the functions referred to in this paragraph being at the eastern end of the Scottish border. There Berwick-on-Tweed is in planning terms the county town of the Scottish county of Berwick and the focal point for all activity on both sides of the lower Tweed.

Before considering the criteria for any new system, it is worth noticing the boundaries adopted by the next series of organizations which turned to regionalism after the Treasury had set up its Standard Units. These were the statutory boards and corporations, for the most part created by the 1945–51 Labour Governments. The regional units they selected are relevant because hospitals, railways, gas, electricity and coal are all deeply connected with the social and economic life of each area and some of these functions (either the execution of them or the exercise of consumers' rights to complain and comment) might well be transferred to top-tier local government units if they were of sufficient size and had sufficient resources.

In the cases of the Hospital Boards, the Railway Boards and the Area Gas and Electricity Boards, the regional bodies were

NORTHERN

YORKSHIRE

LANCASHIRE
AND CHESHIRE

NORTH
MIDLANDS

WEST
MIDLANDS

EASTERN

SOUTH
MID-
LANDS

NORTH
THAMES

SOUTH EASTERN

SOUTH WESTERN

GAS BOARD AREAS

set up as corporate entities by Act of Parliament, while the regional bodies created by the B.B.C., the Coal Board and the Central Electricity Board were all internal administrative decisions. In selecting suitable areas, all these organizations looked primarily to the effective provision of a service. Regions were to be large enough to permit the development of modern methods of production and to carry the best management structure, but some consideration was paid to social and population factors. It was clearly desirable for regions to contain rather than straddle the main conurbations, boundaries were better passing through thinly-inhabited rural areas. While production was the main point for gas and electricity, Hospital Boards were each to have a medical school as a 'focal point' and the Railway Boards based on the British Railway regions were mainly concerned with traffic flows.

The interesting aspect is the degree of similarity that resulted from such divergent points of departure. In example after example, the boundaries of the Northern (Newcastle), North-Western (Lancashire and Cheshire or Manchester), Yorkshire (Leeds), West Midlands (Midlands, Birmingham), East Midlands (Sheffield or North Midland) and South-Western Regions are very much the same. The one outstanding exception among these areas is the Liverpool Hospital Region. All of these patterns also have an East Anglian region but thereafter the uniformity breaks down. In gas there is the small but populous North Thames region with a South Midlands around Oxford. Several have varied south central regions with London being divided in four or five different ways.

In the 1950s, though government departments and the statutory corporations continued to operate their regional organizations and more advisory bodies and joint local authority committees were created, on the whole the emphasis in political and administrative policy was national. There was more interest in dismantling war and post-war machinery and

HOSPITAL REGIONS

little concern with building up new permanent peace-time institutions. Then towards the end of the decade and in the early sixties the atmosphere changed. There was a new concern about varying levels of prosperity in the different parts of Britain. There was a growing realization that all cultural life was not concentrated in London. A series of new and fashionable universities was established in the regions, television companies were formed to cover different parts of Britain and the Beatles made Liverpool the capital of pop music. While Southern, Tyne Tees, Westward, East Anglia and the other television stations ran network programmes, they also had their own time to devote to matters of interest in their own area, to use local talent and to give a local slant to national events.

Finally, in 1965, the Labour Government created six planning regions in all of England except the South-East and constituted Scotland and Wales as planning regions on their own. The South-East was left out as it was not clear whether it should be subdivided. The matter was finally settled by creating two more regions of East Anglia and the remains of the South-East, including Essex, Hertford, Bedfordshire, Buckinghamshire, Oxford, Berkshire and Hampshire. The latter was bigger than the next three regions put together (in terms of population and resources) but there were good reasons (considered below) for the decision. Here then were ten planning regions and the councils each set to work to produce statistical information, economic, land use and transport plans. Only at a later stage did it become clear (see chapter 6 below) that these councils and boards had grave problems in that they were purely advisory: they could neither be sure their plans would be adopted and executed by the local authorities below them nor that they would be endorsed and enforced by the central government above them.

SCOTLAND

Edinburgh

Belfast ▲

Newcastle

NORTHERN

YORKS &
HUMBERSIDE

NORTH WEST

Leeds

Manchester

E. MIDLANDS

Birmingham

Nottingham

E. ANGLIA
Offices in London

WALES

W. MIDLANDS

Cardiff

Bristol

London

SOUTH EAST

SOUTH WEST

● Offices of Economic Planning Councils and Boards   ▲ Economic Council set up by Northern Ireland Government

ECONOMIC PLANNING REGIONS

Population and Rateable Value of the Planning Regions

	Population at June 1967	£,000 Rateable value at April 1967
North	3,329,510	117,020·8
Yorkshire and Humberside	4,782,890	164,388·1
East Midlands	3,295,460	126,183·3
East Anglia	1,611,910	56,276·5
South-East	17,185,550	1,100,446·1
Wales	2,709,930	92,107·6
South-West	3,652,230	139,573·2
West Midlands	5,067,420	204,487·1
North-West	6,755,900	254,546·9
Scotland	5,186,600	142,334·0

But the immediate result was a revival of regionalism and a new set of units. By the early 1960s the *Economist* had brought out its regional scheme, the *Observer* was broadly in agreement, the Acton Society Trust prepared a three-volume study, the Buchanan Report on *Traffic in Towns* came out in favour of large regions and then the policy was adopted as part of the Department of Economic Affairs' implementation of the National Plan and of encouragement of growth. It is not surprising that many of those eager for local government reform pointed out that these units would be suitable as top-tier regions for electoral and administrative purposes, particularly if there was to be an actual devolution of some central government functions.

The Best Boundaries

In selecting the most suitable boundaries for large regions there are two kinds of problems. The first is to decide which is the most important function to which the boundaries suggested

1 CALEDONIA Inverness	9 SEVERN Birmingham
2 CLYDE Glasgow	10 SNOWDON Liverpool
3 LALLANS Edinburgh	11 BRECON Swansea
4 SOLWAY Carlisle	12 COTSWOLD Bristol
5 NORTHUMBRIA Newcastle	13 LYONESSE Plymouth
6 LANCASTER Manchester	14 HAMPTON Southampton
7 YORK York	15 LONDON London
8 WASH Lincoln	16 ANGLIA Norwich

TOWARDS A FEDERAL BRITAIN

Sixteen Large-Scale Regions Proposed by The Economist in its Mark I Plan

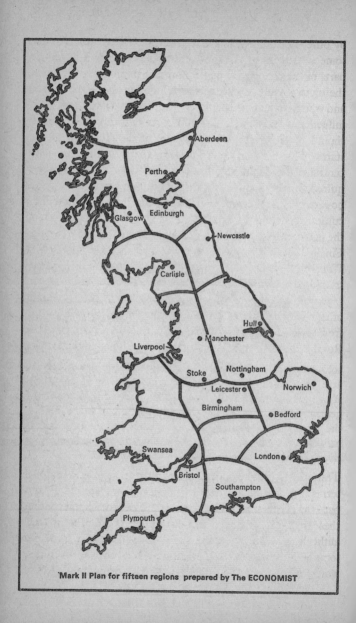

Mark II Plan for fifteen regions prepared by The ECONOMIST

by other functions will have to give way. The second is to find some settlement of the intricate problems created in certain parts of the country by population distribution. Of the latter, the most obvious problem is how London should be treated and whether attempts should be made to cut down its size and influence as against that of the other regions; that is, whether it should be circumscribed or divided or be allowed a special status. This decision determines whether a central or south central region in the area from Oxford to Southampton is required. In the South-West there is a problem of the eastern boundary of any region, while in the North there are the difficulties about the Liverpool-Manchester complex and about the northern and southern boundaries of the Yorkshire Region. Finally, some advocates of large regions have subdivided Wales and Scotland (for instance, the *Economist*), others treating both as units on their old national boundaries.

On the question of functions much depends on the degree of devolution that is contemplated. Two points clearly emerge from the evidence of the Department of Economic Affairs to the Royal Commission on Local Government. The first is that the

solution of the economic and environmental problems likely to arise in the next 15 to 20 years ... has been felt to require a strategic regional planning framework ... covering *inter alia* the general population and employment pattern for the region, the needs and priorities in the development of major communications and the major land use and social infrastructure objectives.

Thus any national planning has to be translated into regional terms and laid out in detail in terms of local priorities and patterns of investment if it is to work. The second point is that these regional strategies will determine the policy of local authorities on land use, the siting of industry, the level and location of house building, overspill, urban renewal, amenities, water and drainage. So if there is to be a meaningful degree of local choice and decision on these important matters which affect so many citizens, the unit chosen must be capable of conducting this strategic regional planning. To settle for smaller units or unsuitable units would be to leave all the most important issues affecting the lives of the local communities in the hands of the central government and probably there would still have to be advice tendered by nominated regional councils.

But to select economic and land use planning as the key function by which to determine the most suitable of the possible large scale regions does not conclude the matter. The D.E.A. indicated that this could possibly be done by authorities covering smaller areas than the present planning councils, providing these present planning regions were not split into more than four units in each case. This is almost certainly too many, but there is a range from the sixteen regions put forward by the *Economist* to the ten present planning regions which would all be capable of such functions. If the sixteen are compared with the ten, it will be seen that the differences arise from different solutions to the particular boundary problems mentioned above. The larger number of regions comes from dividing the South-East into four units and subdividing Wales and Scotland. The other regions – one in the North-East, a larger Lancashire and a South-Western region – retain much the same shape. Moreover, planning is possible at slightly different levels. For instance, in Scotland the overall picture was worked out by the Scottish Planning Council and published in *The Scottish Economy 1965–1970* (Cmnd. 2864), but this series of objectives, regional levels of investment and population targets was then given to four subordinate advisory committees (the North-East, Tayside, the Borders and the South-West) while the Highland section was left to the Highland Development Board. It was open to these subordinate bodies to raise questions of local application. There is also the case that Wales in planning terms has two sections, one linked south with the Severn, the other north to Merseyside. Finally, London remains a headache for though the G.L.C. is, in a sense, the only current attempt at regional government, the report of the Greater London Group entitled *The Lessons of the London Reforms* points out that the present area is too restricted and that 'there is a case for a wider area for the exercise of planning and highway functions but it is difficult to delimit such an area within the South-East Planning Region'. The Greater London Group was not able to come to a unanimous recommendation on this point and left the argument open by putting forward two alternatives: Scheme A with a single elected regional authority for the whole of the South-East but excluding the 'counter-magnet' areas of future intensive growth, and Scheme B which contained four regions radiating out from London and including the 'counter-magnet' areas.

In view of these complexities, it is best to leave these different possibilities open till the situation in Wales, Scotland and London have been more thoroughly discussed in chapters 6 and 7, as other factors in the political or administrative spheres may then emerge which will point definitely in favour of one or other of the alternatives possible in these three areas. But it can be accepted that among the advocates of the large-region solution there is substantial agreement on size and boundaries for seven of the regions of England.

Functions

Units of this size could clearly handle all the functions listed on pages 49–50 above down to number 27. Many tasks at present divided between both these authorities and *ad hoc* agencies could be given to large regions with only a few guide lines laid down by the central government.

It has been argued that the key function on which the

preference for large regions is chiefly based is that of economic and land use planning. But here, as with many other functions, there is no neat dividing line between the aspects that must remain with the central government and those that can be devolved. For instance, with more sophisticated and regionally collected statistics, the regional authorities could and should make claims for their regions, but it would be up to the central government to see that the total requirements for capital and the total population movements made sense from a national point of view. If regions in the North and West calculate they will lose by emigration to the South-East, that region must take more account of the fact and plan accordingly. The adjudicator in any case of dispute must be the central government. Regions may decide that certain lines of industrial development are most profitable or helpful in their areas, but if there are to be only three aluminium smelters and each is to be subsidized by the central government, it is the latter which must finally decide on their location. Similarly, while several regions may put up claims for new cities on the Severn, the Solway or Humberside, only the central government can settle where such a specially large injection of capital is to be made.

On the other hand, the task of shopping for smaller industries where no special subsidy is required, selecting the sites for new towns the cost of which can be met out of the regional budget, and the choice of roads to develop, are all matters for the region itself. An example of the kind of decision that should be devolved is the number, siting and building of advance factories. At present the central government allots such factories to the various regions. The regional planning councils and boards then suggest specific sites which have to be approved by the Board of Trade. Then Treasury sanction is given and the task of building the factory returns to the Board of Trade operating through an agency which builds and manages industrial estates.

In a devolved system with large units, this could be greatly simplified, the only central government decision being the level of industrial investment to be allowed to the regional authority in question. The latter could then decide how much of this was to go into advance factories and could site, build and manage them itself. Together with the power to build advance factories and to establish industrial estates, there should be the power to draw up urban redevelopment schemes, to take the major decisions about zoning land, to carry through overspill programmes and construct housing estates. It is arguable that some powers to construct houses and possibly all management of local authority housing should be allocated to second-tier authorities, but the larger projects involving the decanting of population and the clearance and reconstruction of large areas must be a task for the top-tier units.

These regions could also be responsible for education, though they would have to comply with such basic national requirements as that education must be compulsory up to a certain age and must be available free of charge. A national authority might also have to handle agreements with the churches on religious schools and instruction. Thereafter all education could be left to the regional authority. Some of those writing on this subject have exempted universities, but without any good reason. Indeed, one of the pressing problems at present is how to ensure adequate control of forty-three institutions through a single part-time body of academics, the University Grants Committee. Many have pointed out that a proper knowledge of each university's needs and possibilities is impossible on this basis and the result is more form-filling and control by officials. At the same time, at its current cost, university education cannot expect to be totally unconnected with further education, technical education and the many other bodies providing skilled training for those over eighteen. Regional U.G.C.s given a sum of money could allocate it with much more intimate knowledge of each university and could see that there was a fuller integration with the other educational institutions in the area.

Such large regions could, but need not, manage all aspects of school education. They could run secondary education, teacher training, further education, the general supervision of curricula, and the recruitment, pay and standards of the teaching profession, while primary education could be left to second-tier local authorities.

If the production of gas and electricity were organized in the same regions, investment and pricing policies in these industries would still be a matter for a national ministry of fuel and power, but consumer-council status could be given to the elected regional assemblies. These assemblies, which should be allowed to nominate one or two members to the regional gas and electricity boards, could maintain a much better watch over consumers' interests, and the public would turn to their regional representative on this as on all other local government questions.

Obviously an important function would be transport control. All the powers presently given to Passenger Transport Authorities by the 1968 Transport Bill would pass to the regional authorities with the addition of powers to construct all roads, bridges and ferries, though there would have to be acceptance of a national government directive about the total amount permitted in investment in roads in any one year. The present elaborate process of seeking central government consent at a large number of stages in main road construction would then become unnecessary as the regions would be large enough to maintain a full and competent staff of road engineers, surveyors and architects. These powers over roads could be complemented by giving the regional assemblies a voice on the management boards of the relevant section of British Rail and complete powers to construct and control airports in the region, apart from certain specially designated 'national airports' which would be serving much more than the needs of the region in question.

There could be a considerable devolution of the powers of the Ministry of Agriculture and Fisheries to inspect, give advice on and approve schemes of farm improvement. This is already done for Scotland (population five million) by the Scottish Office and could well be performed in each of the regions, though the collection of statistics and negotiation of annual price guarantees and production grants would remain with the Ministry in Whitehall. At the same time the major *ad hoc* bodies affecting food production and the use of the countryside could be abolished or divided and their tasks given to the regions. Forestry, for instance, could be divided in this way, as could the work of the Herring Board and White Fish Authority. The allocation of land for amenities, open spaces and green belts could well be devolved, and the Countryside Commissions, the National Parks authorities and the various Tourists Boards wound up and their powers regionalized. These functions, together with the work of River Boards and River Pollution and Water Resources Boards, could in every case, except possibly one or two water schemes in Wales, also be given to the regional authorities. The result would be a comprehensive responsibility for the supervision of all land uses from agriculture to holiday purposes, including coastal preservation and fishing, the development of natural resources, and the encouragement of tourism.

The services concerned with welfare could be organized in the most satisfactory manner suggested by current experience. For instance, if hospitals were grouped in the same regions, the tri-partite structure of the Health Service, with all the anomalies it creates, could be abandoned. The regional ministry or department of health could run hospitals, organize the general practitioners in groups and combine both with the present local authority health services. This would permit the linking of practices with district nurses and health visitors and the connection of each group with a given specialist hospital and a local convalescent centre. The Health Service would thus look after all aspects of health and would be under the control of an elected body, with the hospital doctors and general practitioners advising about their aspects of the service but not being in executive positions. In general, this is desirable, as it is never very satisfactory to have a service intended for the public run completely by the professional persons concerned. If the professionals are in charge, there is a gradual but definite tendency for the convenience and criteria of those running the service to come first and the customers or patients to come second. In addition preventive medicine could be given its proper place and the combined control of health would include supervision of the various forms of regulation covered at present in food and milk administration and the regulation of drugs.

All other welfare services, including the Home Office functions of probation, child care, remand homes and the trial and supervision of juvenile offenders could be handled by a single department as was recommended by the Kilbrandon Report in Scotland and is being considered by the Seebohm Committee in England. In time, it might be possible to move to a more positive approach to welfare, where the social workers had allotted areas which they visited to find out if all living there were being properly catered for, to ensure that the public knew of the various services and that these were being administered in a correct and equitable fashion.

While there is a strong case for a single national police force, ten to sixteen forces for the U.K. would be a reduction on the present number and there is little doubt that forces of this size could be efficiently run. Fire services could be organized on the same basis. Control of these services, particularly that of the police is somewhat obscure and while the methods and discipline of these forces are clearly a matter for their professional commander, the overall relations of the forces with the public and decisions as to the functions of the forces should be clearly placed in the hands of a minister or chairman selected by the regional assembly.

There remains the regulatory functions of registration of births, marriages and deaths and the provision of such services as libraries and museums. As these assemblies would already possess such wide powers to promote development and welfare throughout the regions, the final provision (apart from financial powers, to be discussed later) would be to accept the recommendation of the Committee on Management and award them a 'general competence' to do anything not prohibited by law which would be in the interests of the local community. With this degree of devolution and concentration of powers, at present diffused over many bodies, in the sole hands of the top-tier authorities, these large regions would have genuine scope to act on behalf of their area, to give those living there a sense of control over their environment and to develop along lines which differed, in accordance with local needs, from the pattern pursued in neighbouring regions. It would reduce the need for Whitehall supervision to an absolute minimum and free central government from a mass of its detailed work, leaving it to manage national policies, to think ahead and work out the best overall lines for Britain's economy, its social services, defence and external policies.

Problems of large-region solution

The first difficulty is that, as in the case of city regions, second-tier units would be required and it is hard to decide on the appropriate size and functions for them. In the one current regional government operating in Britain, the G.L.C., the answer has been to have a second tier of thirty-two boroughs with populations ranging from 147,000 to 345,000. In this case, the boroughs are the primary units of local government and perform all functions except those which can be effectively managed by the G.L.C., particularly housing, health and welfare services, aspects of planning, roads, libraries and parks, while the twenty outer London boroughs control education and the School Medical Service. On the whole, the system is working fairly well, but for a variety of reasons which are largely peculiar to London. For example, the boundary of Greater London is fairly clear and though local loyalties exist within London, these did not interfere in any serious way with the framing of the borough boundaries. As a result it was not difficult to produce thirty-two fairly compact boroughs of a size and wealth equal to the tasks given to second-tier authorities.

This pattern could not be repeated easily elsewhere for several reasons. In the first place, in the other conurbations, there are much stronger ties of loyalty to sub-sections which may have had a separate existence for decades, if not centuries. Someone living in Salford might not readily accept borough status within a Manchester Greater Council or someone from Motherwell in a Greater Glasgow. Secondly, if the boroughs or second-tier units are to have an equivalent level of population and resources, in many cases they would have to include large areas of countryside and so become highly dispersed, in places being as large as some of the city regions examined in chapter 3. Units of this size would, for example, include the entire Highlands of Scotland or three or four counties in north Wales, areas far too broad to be effective as second-tier units or requiring a third-tier local authority which would add greatly to the complexity of the pattern of local government.

One of the main objectives of a thorough-going reform is to

produce a simple, intelligible arrangement, so that the citizen turns naturally to a local council on matters than affect the locality, to a regional body on questions concerning the broader patterns of local development and services, and to the central government on issues of national policy. It is doubtful whether the second-tier pattern now adopted in London would work outside heavily populated areas such as the South-East and the industrial Midlands, and it is arguable that even in London, it would have been better had more powers been given to the G.L.C. rather than to the boroughs. It would probably be most effective if the functions described on pages 85-91 and listed as 1 to 28 on pages 49-50 were allocated to the main regional authority, leaving functions 29 to 41 to second-tier authorities. But these tasks are not very exciting, the only one of real significance being the building of housing schemes (as opposed to major overspill and redevelopment) and the management of housing. If second-tier units are largely rural and are kept to a smallish area, such as the size of present counties of some 40,000 inhabitants, this would be sufficient responsibility. But the problem remains as to whether cities, Manchester and Liverpool for instance, now exercising far wider powers, would be content either to be subdivided into boroughs or to remain as united second-tier authorities with these restricted functions.

The alternative is to avoid the present policy of devising one uniform system for the whole country. While large and powerful second-tier authorities might be most effective in London, it is accepted, for example, that outer boroughs are responsible for education whereas central boroughs are not. A similar distinction could be drawn if the Greater London Council were extended over the South-East, and where there were largely rural second-tier units these could be allocated tasks suitable for their size and resources. In short, the powers and extent of second-tier units could be left to each regional council and each might have special cases meriting distinct treatment. The present attempt to get all bodies with the same title to perform the same functions has great weaknesses, as has the policy of fixing an optimum size in population terms for any function and insisting on a geographical unit large enough to encompass this number of people. Thus the Scottish Office, with some fixed target in mind for the numbers needed to constitute a Water Board, found that the islands of Orkney and Shetland had a mere 35,000 people and insisted on combining them for the purposes of freshwater supplies with mainland counties from which they are separated by an open stretch of ocean. On the same principle the headquarters of the Shetland Fire Service is in Inverness, some two hundred miles away as the crow flies.

It may be objected that the history of delegation in the present local government system is not an altogether happy one and that the varied pattern that would result might make local government hard to understand. On the other hand, people in Devon or Somerset cannot be expected to know much about how local government works in London. What is necessary is not that there should be a comprehensible national pattern which, when understood for one area, can be applied to another. The important point is that the system should make sense to those who live under it, and that a second-tier unit such as Plymouth or Exeter should not be restricted to the functions which could be properly performed by other second-tier units near by, such as Penzance, St Just and St Ives. If this solution were adopted, it would be important to leave its arrangement and regulation entirely to the regional authority and for the central government to take no part in preparing, authorizing or supervising the system devised by each region.

The second main problem of the large-region solution and the one most often quoted against it is that regions of this size are 'not local government'. In part, this objection arises from too much familiarity with the existing British system and an assumption that anything much larger than a big county or borough is therefore in some sense moving into another category. If all that is not central government is defined as local government the semantic problem is overcome, but there is still a real feeling that the word 'local' ought to mean something small, with the council chambers and the nearest elected councillor close at hand. Pressed to give content to the objection, those who make it tend to argue that the average elector wants to know his councillor and to be able to call on him. Councils, it is said, will attract even fewer candidates if much travelling to meetings is involved and there is even less public interest in or attachment to big artificial regions. Also officials ought to be able to know the area intimately and appreciate all local circumstances down to matters of detail if services are to meet the needs of the citizens, a large-scale regional government being for most people as remote as Whitehall.

It is worth looking at these objections in turn. There is no positive evidence about the attitude of potential candidates to such large units of local government and much would depend on the way they were constituted and organized. If the powers were as extensive as those suggested above and if the committee system were established, there would be great attractions in serving on such bodies. Given freedom to make a real difference to the development and standard of services offered in a sizeable portion of the country, and the attractive possibility of becoming the Prime Minister of the North-East or of Wales, the whole attitude to service in local government might well change. With powers of the kind indicated, the head of a regional council would be as important a figure as a cabinet minister and service on regional councils might, as with state governors in the U.S.A. and *Land* leaders in Germany, become a recognized path towards national leadership. The evidence suggests that once there is a real chance to make a difference to policies that affect people, candidates of the highest quality come forward. In the first flush of regional planning in 1965, when it was thought that these councils would be powerful and effective bodies, many very able people in each region showed a positive desire to serve. Similarly, some Conservatives with a bent for action who failed to get re-elected in 1966 but were swept on to the G.L.C. in the next year, found that they had more interesting work and more influence than in their days as backbenchers at Westminster.

It is also important that the gap between those serving in local politics and those coming forward at the national level should be largely removed. If the country faces prolonged periods when one party is in power, the opposition is in danger of losing men whose chief interest is administration and of losing therefore all experience of government. The Conservatives were in office for thirteen years between 1951 and 1964 and it seems likely (in 1968) that any government which can solve the balance of payments problem and induce steady growth will secure its position in power for a very long time. Under these circumstances, it is extremely important for opposition leaders or future leaders to be able to take the lead in those regions which will remain solidly Conservative or Labour whatever the complexion of national politics. In British terms, it is hard to understand what kept the German Social Democratic Party together and an effective force during thirty years in opposition. The answer is that it was always in power in Saxony or the City of Berlin, and experience of the kind enjoyed by Willy Brandt or Helmut Schmidt would certainly have been useful to Labour leaders, only two of whom had ever sat in a Cabinet before, when Labour was elected in 1964.

Thus there seems to be no ground for the argument that adequate councillors would not come forward in a large-region system, though there might be some reasons for fearing this if the large regions were as hemmed in by Whitehall controls and as cluttered with detailed committee work as the present county councils.

From the point of view of the public, the argument that this would not be 'local' government is curious. There would be more councillors elected for such large regions than there are M.P.s and few people have argued that the active local M.P. is unavailable or unknown. With electorates averaging perhaps 20,000 in a constituency, the councillors could hold surgeries and be telephoned or seen twice as easily as the M.P. What matters to the public is not that the councillor lives next door but that if one drives a short distance to see him or telephones him, he can actually do something about the complaint. The public's disillusion with local government and reluctance to find out the name of the local councillor or to contact him is a realistic appreciation of how much he is likely to be able to do for them. If there were a council with the breadth of action envisaged here, it would receive considerable publicity, the members would become known in their constituencies, and with modern means of communication there would be little difficulty for electors in making contact with them.

It is sometimes said that these large regions are artificial and lack any sense of community or loyalty among their inhabitants. This is only true in part, for there is a feeling of pride in being a Londoner and conversely local pride grows the further one gets from London. No one can now deny that great enthusiasm is aroused by the notion of a measure of self-government for Scotland and for Wales. Indeed, one of the reasons why Westminster politicians resist the idea of a single-unit government in both these cases is the shrewd suspicion that the Prime Minister or Chairman of these councils or assemblies would create far more interest and draw more support than any local M.P. There is fairly strong sentiment also in the North-East, the North-West, in Yorkshire and the South-West. The only areas which lack such a feeling are those which are fairly close to London and where there has so far been no history of common action or organization. But it would be hard to demonstrate that an East or West Midlands region would have less sense of unity than some of the present rather amorphous counties (Northamptonshire or Warwickshire) or some of the proposed city regions for this area.

The factors that have taken the glamour out of local government have been its powerlessness, complexity, lack of scope for the young, active, ambitious councillor, and the continual supervision by Whitehall. This is why that reform of local government which allows the maximum transfer of coherent important powers to the new authorities, the one that allows the sharpest break with present methods of management, is the one most likely to produce public interest, loyalty and participation. The fact that so many services are best administered or can only be planned on a regional basis will be the greatest help in creating units that will build up an active political life of their own.

Chapter 6
Existing Forms of Regionalism

It would be comforting to think that if it could be demonstrated that a certain solution would produce the most vital and viable elected pattern of local government, this would be the end of the argument. This might appear to follow from the apparent consensus that local government reform is desirable. But, as has been said, this agreement conceals total disagreement about the degree of independence local government should have, about the extent to which it is desirable that policies should be modified to suit each region and about how far centres of political power outside Whitehall-Westminster are to be welcomed. Part of the attraction of the thirty to forty city region solution for Whitehall is precisely that it would make any devolution of further powers to local government impossible; the regional machinery of the central departments and the planning staffs of the regional boards would all still be required as part of central government.

In addition to the attitude of the central civil service, many M.P.s and ministers (including shadow ministers on the opposition front bench) would be very worried at the thought that Westminster could not immediately order all local authorities to follow a special policy in the organization of health or of education. Britain has become so centralized and so monolithic in governmental terms that there is tremendous reluctance to delegate tasks, or give other bodies a chance to act differently and quickly, accepting that this may produce some contrasts and complaints. Thus, a Ministry may set up a series of regional controllers to adopt policies to suit each area, but once an M.P. rises in the House and says 'case X was treated this way in Cornwall and now I have evidence that identical case Y was handled a little differently in Leicestershire', there is consternation. It is assumed that this is a weakness. It is not supposed to be a proper answer to say 'but Cornwall is not Leicestershire' or 'this is because regional controllers are allowed to interpret these powers as seems best in their area' or 'the provision of machinery to review all cases throughout Britain in order to be sure that similar cases are always treated in exactly the same way means centralization, excessive delays and enormous bureaucratic cost'. Even less is it regarded as a proper answer to say that it is not always certain that there is only one way of carrying out a policy and it is desirable to see different methods in practice.

This desire for uniformity, this fear of the political consequences of diversity and of an element of devolution of actual power is the major explanation for the myriad controls imposed on local government. It is sometimes claimed that they exist to be of aid to the weaker, less expert authorities, but in fact the same controls are imposed on those that are large, rich and well-staffed, such as the G.L.C. The idea of division of powers and that the governments' writ might not run throughout the country on all issues is really foreign to much political thinking in Britain. There is, therefore, a real danger that whatever reforms are carried through in local government they will be largely of a tidying-up or rationalizing type and that any proposals will deliberately avoid the creation of bodies with a genuine degree of independence. If, then, after all this is done there is still no revival of interest and involvement, it will be said that it only goes to show that no one wants local democracy just as, after some rather direction-less tinkering with Parliamentary procedure in 1966–7 had failed to make a marked improvement in the conduct of business in Westminster, it was alleged that Parliamentary reform was a failure.

In order to appreciate these dangers and to see the direction in which changes have gone so far, it is worth examining the steps already taken towards regionalism.

The Regional Planning Councils and Boards

The Labour Party had talked about the need for regional planning before it came to power in 1964. In the debate on the Buchanan Report, *Traffic in Towns*, Mr Michael Stewart argued in favour of regional bodies which would consult with the local authorities. He emphasized that he did not consider 'trying to build up the regional organization by expanding the size and powers of existing local authorities. We must have devolution from the central government, not an attempt to enlarge the areas and powers of local authorities'. After the election the Department of Economic Affairs was created, and part of its task was to supervise and receive reports from the regions. In each region the officials of the Whitehall Departments allocated to the region were to meet as a board under the chairmanship of a D.E.A. official and collect regional statistics and prepare regional plans. Then regional councils were appointed, one third of the members being drawn from the local authorities, one third from industry and the unions, and the rest from prominent institutions in the region such as the local universities. In Scotland the Secretary of State and in Wales the Minister of State became the Chairmen, but elsewhere prominent local figures were appointed.

The precise roles of these two bodies, the councils and the boards, were not thought out. For instance, if a problem arose in housing or in fuel and power, did the regional controller take it first to the Board or the Council or did he start by consulting

Whitehall? And if his Ministry took one view and the Board and Council took another, how was the dispute to be settled? In the case of the councils, they were composed of reputable but busy men with established positions in other concerns. They met once a month or thereabouts but their task was not clear. They were not appointed as representatives of local bodies and they were not allowed to report the proceedings of the councils to the other regional or local bodies on which they served. On the other hand, they were not intended to do executive work as the meetings were rare and there was little research staff. It would appear that the chief function of the councils has been to consider and endorse plans or proposals put on their agenda by the planning boards. Once their conclusions had been published, their task was to 'collaborate with the local authorities upon which must rest so much of the responsibility for implementing the regional plans'. But those aspects of their proposals which were the responsibility of the central departments could, presumably, be implemented by the departmental civil servants who sat on the boards.

The central control of the various tasks given to the regional boards and councils is spread among a large number of ministries. While overall regional strategy remains with the D.E.A., the Treasury has tightened its hold on investment and the Board of Trade still controls the location of advance factories, as well as the award of loans, grants and Industrial Development Certificates (that is, permission to build) to new industry. Physical as opposed to economic planning is (since the abolition of the Ministry of Land and Natural Resources in 1967) the task of the Ministry of Housing and Local Government, while the Ministries of Agriculture, Fisheries and Food, of Transport and of Fuel and Power all have important parts to play. It is significant that regional planning has worked best in Scotland where there is a regional minister and department which combines the duties of nine English Ministries. Thus,

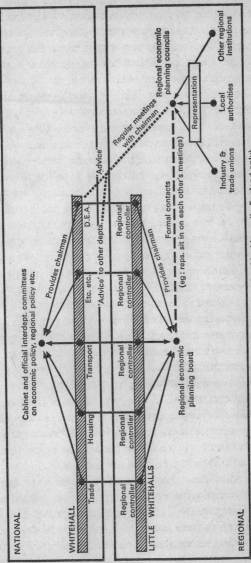

The Structure of Regional Planning Machinery (in England only)

NATIONAL

WHITEHALL

Trade | Housing | Transport | Etc. etc. | D.E.A.

Provides chairman

'Advice' to other depts.

Cabinet and official interdept. committees on economic policy, regional policy etc.

Provides chairman

LITTLE WHITEHALLS

Regional controller | Regional controller | Regional controller | Regional controller | Regional controller

Regional economic planning board

REGIONAL

Advice

Regular meetings with chairman

Regional economic planning councils

Formal contacts
(eg : reps. sit in on each other's meetings)

Representation

Other regional institutions

Local authorities

Industry & trade unions

there is an official level at which matters that are normally inter-departmental can be settled in the Scottish Office without the time taken and divergent criteria which can arise when an issue has to go up to different ministers in Whitehall. Trouble on these questions usually arises in Scotland only when the question in dispute is between the Scottish Office and other ministries with Scottish responsibilities.

The councils and boards started work in 1965 (with the exceptions of the two appointed later) in a blaze of public acclaim and enthusiasm. A series of plans was produced and the Government gave its backing to a policy of regional development. This has caused some confusion, for the phrase 'regional planning' or 'regional policies' has been used in two different ways. One meaning refers to the attempt to raise wages, reduce unemployment and increase investment in certain regions by means of investment grants, a regional employment premium, special aid with the construction of infrastructure and the refusal of Industrial Development Certificates to firms wishing to expand in the more prosperous regions. This policy has been a success in that the level of unemployment in the less buoyant regions has not been as high a proportion of the U.K. total in the 1967 recession as it was in 1963. Wage rates have caught up. Thirty-six per cent of new factory construction was in these regions in 1967 as opposed to twenty-five per cent in 1962. At the same time, the very success of these policies in an almost static economy has led to actual closures of factories in the South-East, a net loss of population in the G.L.C. area of 87,000 in 1965–6 and some anxiety in the so-called 'grey areas' next to the development areas.

As a result, there has been some criticism of regional economic policy in this sense. But in this sense it is a national policy which has no need of local democratic bodies. This book is considering 'regional planning' as one of the functions to be awarded to large-scale local government units in all parts of

Britain, in those selected as the beneficiaries of regional economic development as well as in those being held under some
restraint. The argument here is that while it is a national task
to draw up overall policies of industrial redistribution, to
determine the targets and techniques to be used and to decide
on major developments such as new cities, it should be the task
of regional democratic machinery first to comment on these
proposals, then to work out their application in terms of regional priorities and finally to do the job, with all its side effects on
housing, transport, amenities and so on.

All that exists at present of regional planning in this second
institutional sense is the work of the nominated councils and
the official boards and these have run into serious difficulties,
as can be seen from the statements and resignations (or
threats of resignation) of prominent members. The cause of
these difficulties is that the original failure to think out the
position of the councils and boards meant a consequent failure
to give them adequate powers either to deal with local authorities or to re-arrange Whitehall departmental procedures so as
to permit regional advice to have a proper effect. One problem
that appeared almost at once was that the councils (except in
the case of Scotland) lacked adequate staff to collect the information needed. Secondly, it has become apparent that the
regional civil servants on the boards are not in a satisfactory
position. Often very junior, their loyalty is not to the region
but to their department, and their objective is not to win praise
for putting the region's case possibly against the views of their
masters in Whitehall but to please these masters so that they
can return from exile in the provinces. Again the only cases in
which this does not apply, at least over a number of branches
of the government, is in Scotland and Wales, where there are
regional departments of state with a full career structure,
though even in these cases there are some inhibitions (discussed in the next section). Thus, where Whitehall Depart-

ments have different criteria, these are not being reconciled in the interests of each particular region but are being fought out and won in the trenches of Whitehall. In practice, when this happened, the Chairmen of the various councils had to make the matter into a semi-political issue and go to London and fight it out with the relevant minister. Mrs Castle as Minister of Transport was the only minister to grasp the point of regional councils, to have regular meetings with their chairmen and to listen to them. On the other hand, the Ministry of Housing and Local Government had fought to prevent land use planning being given to the councils (whether it was so given has always remained obscure) and refused to consult. So did the Ministries of Education and of Fuel and Power. One crisis came when the North-East Planning Council had been preparing the introduction of new industry into a declining coal field and the provision of re-training facilities. Mr Dan Smith, the Chairman, working from a Ministry of Fuel and Power programme, visited each pit to set out the position. After one such visit when he had told the men that the pit had two years to run, its closure was announced by the Ministry for three months ahead (and, as it happened, two weeks before Christmas). This was prevented only by a public threat of resignation, but the point was that the Ministry in London had never contemplated the need to consult either the Planning Board or the Council before revising the programme of closures which it had given them.

Those chairmen of economic planning councils who were more interested in the sophisticated aspects of planning were also dissatisfied. The statistics of regional production were not available. Worse, they found no central attempt to draw their plans together and see that the ten sets of objectives added up to totals that made sense from a national point of view. Some complained that the Scottish Plan which aimed at ending net emigration from Scotland by 1970 was unrealistic and that this target could not be altered to a realistic one for political reasons. As a result the population inflows which the other regions could expect were not satisfactory. Also, after studying local conditions, some councils wanted to alter the balance of investment (not the total) in their region. The North-West, for instance, declared that it would prefer more spent on roads even if it meant some reduction in the expenditure on education. But they found that each department had fought for its annual budget with the Treasury and to offer to spend less on eduction meant that that sum was lost without any guarantee that an equivalent would be added to the road programme for the region.

Not only do these experiences show that Whitehall had in no way altered its vertical structure to meet the horizontal groupings of departments in the regions, but when the resulting quarrels led to arguments between councils and ministers, the unsatisfactory position of those nominated to these councils became very evident. If the councils decide simply to endorse Whitehall decisions, there is no point in their existence. If, on the other hand, they try to take a stand, there is great alarm and no satisfactory answer to the Government's retort 'Who do you think you are to object, who put you on the Council?' Thus, Professor Tress objected to cuts in investment being imposed on the South-West but achieved little. Professor Nevin resigned from the Welsh Council and Professor Carter from the North-West because they were dissatisfied with their positions, and Mr Dan Smith threatened to give up the chairmanship of the North-East if London did not pay more attention to regional views and the need for regional consultations. This is a basic problem. The councils represent no one so they can scarcely press hard on the central government. In general, their work has had little or no publicity, their meetings are in private, the arguments are not reported in the Press and, as there is little concrete evidence of their activities, they have accumulated no measure of public support on which they could lean.

This weakness cuts both ways. Not only is there little leverage against Whitehall but the councils face equal or greater difficulties in persuading the local authorities to adopt their proposals. At first regional plans were largely collections of data showing the implications of the National Plan for each region. While plans were in this form there was little trouble with local authorities. But as the plans became more sophisticated, they were worked out in detail for sub-sections of the areas covered by the councils in a manner which required the local authorities' active co-operation, as the latter had to alter their development plans and agree to make compulsory purchase orders. Also, planning spread to regions such as the South-East where economic growth was not so important, the main issues being urban redevelopment and the dispersal of population, for which land use planning is essential. These developments could cause difficulties within a region as when Severnside planning seemed to contradict the notion that the South-West on its existing boundaries was a sensible unit. But more often the trouble came with the local authorities. One of the most advanced exercises of the kind described was when the section of the Scottish Plan for the Central Borders was translated into a careful programme of investment in roads, houses, industry and amenities up to the year 1980 by a team led by Professor Johnson-Marshall (land use) and Professor Wolfe (economic development). This report was hailed with enthusiasm throughout Scotland but to carry it out required an elaborate series of decisions by three county councils each armed with the planning powers of the 1947 Town and Country Planning Act. In July 1968 one of the county councils, Roxburghshire, moved partly by land owners' distaste for development, partly by the irritation of small boroughs who felt they got too little out of the plan, simply rejected it. They refused to acquire the land for the first stage (a housing estate at Gala-shiels) or to give planning permission for the second stage (a new town at St Boswells). Thus, unless the county council changes its mind, the whole plan has come to nothing.

A rather different type of problem, but one that could have the same result, has arisen in the South-East where the G.L.C. has set up a Standing Conference on London Regional Planning with more research staff and actual authority than the South-East Planning Council. The local authorities in the West Midlands led by Birmingham have followed suit with their own standing conference. As a result of these tendencies on the part of both Whitehall and the larger local authorities to carry on in the old ways and sometimes to pay mere lip-service to the idea of regional consultation and decision-making, some of the more active council members have concluded that regional planning is dead, and that all that remains is consent to a formal burial.

Certain conclusions seem inescapable after this experience. The first is that while the nation may aim at overall targets in a number of spheres – or simply accept that certain changes must come – these cannot be worked out in all their local implica-tions and all the investment cannot be managed by Whitehall, without leading too often to blunders of the kind made in deciding to site an airport (a national decision) at Stansted. If the detailed application of national changes is to be worked out locally and the results are to be put into practice, the body that does this must be able in some measure to claim authority, to have some independence as against the central government, and this is only possible if it is elected. Secondly, it must also have the capacity to carry out the policy itself and this implies the possession of executive powers. To carry through these reforms and create elected regional councils which would also be responsible for executing the main lines of their plans would instil life and vigour into a level of government which is essential but is ineffective at present because the councils float in a limbo between an overpowerful, vertically departmentalized central government and a mass of varied, weak, over-supervised local authorities.

Administrative Devolution:
The Scottish Office

It would seem to be accepted that some regional co-ordination and administration is both inevitable and desirable. If the planning boards and planning councils have run into difficulties partly because regional controllers in each ministry tend to look first to their superiors in Whitehall, it may be argued that the answer is to set up either a ministry for each region or a single ministry responsible for all regional development. Sir Keith Joseph, the Conservative Minister of Housing and Local Government, in 1964 gave a lecture to the Royal Institute of Public Administration and said: 'Regional plans, yes; regional development, yes; but these do not necessarily involve regional government in the sense of regional representative councils. What they do involve is strong regional arms of central government and a reorganized more effective local government.' This was said before there had been any proper experience of regional planning machinery and it is quite possible that those who appreciate the need for decentralized decision-taking in certain fields, but who also dislike any extension of democratic control, might regard administrative devolution as a solution. This is certainly the view of Mr William Ross, the Secretary of State for Scotland, and a number of Welsh politicians feel that, provided there was a Ministry for Wales with powers as extensive as those of the Scottish Office, they would be entirely satisfied.

It is, therefore, worth examining the operation of the Scottish Office to see if the weakness of the planning boards and councils are removed when many regional tasks are given to a single ministry and when it also has executive powers. To appreciate the structure of the Scottish Office, it should be noted that it was built up piecemeal as the central government began to undertake regulatory functions. The first special administrative provision was the Board of Supervision for the Poor Law formed in 1845, to be followed by the General Board of Commissioners in Lunacy in 1857, the Scottish Education Department (as a committee of the Privy Council) in 1872, the Prison Commissioners in 1877 and the Fishery Board in 1882. Three years later, in 1885, Lord Rosebery became the first Secretary for Scotland. Gradually the series of *ad hoc* boards and commissions grew till reorganizations in 1928 and 1939 grouped the more specifically Scottish functions in four Civil Service departments under a Secretary of State, while those offices and boards administering a national service remained the responsibility of the appropriate U.K. Minister. There was a readjustment in 1962 when the Home and Health Departments of the Scottish Office amalgamated and at the same time shed some of their functions to the new Development Department.

The present structure is shown in the chart on pages 114-15 with a list of the principal U.K. ministries that are active in Scotland on the left. The right hand column lists the five Scottish Ministers and two law officers who supervise the four departments and law offices located in Edinburgh and known collectively as St Andrew's House. Liaison between Scottish and U.K. Ministries is managed by personal contacts at ministerial and official levels, helped by certain inter-departmental committees which are listed in the centre. Over several decades this fairly tidy ministerial system has been hedged around with new *ad hoc* authorities, those operating throughout the U.K. (but sometimes with their Scottish sections responsible to the Secretary of State) being listed on the left, the others on the right being peculiar to Scotland. Local authorities in the usual way act as agents for and in cooperation with both U.K. and Scottish departments and there is a Local Government Division in the Development Department. A White Paper published in July 1963 on *The Modernization of Local Government in Scotland* (Cmnd. 2067) complained that the local authorities were both too small and varied too much in size and resources to manage all the functions required of them, but there was no reconsideration of their powers or of their relations with St Andrew's House.

In reviewing this experiment in administrative devolution, a number of tests have to be applied. The first is whether being closer in geographical terms to the field of operation, and having a smaller population to deal with, enables the Department to know more about its task and its subject and so to have a better intelligence service. Secondly, there is the question of how far being under a single minister permits swifter co-ordination and action. Then there is the test of whether national policies when applied through St Andrew's House can be and are adapted to any particular circumstances in Scotland which do not arise elsewhere, and finally, does this remove the grievance about remote government? Is the electorate conscious of a difference, a greater sense of local flavour about the administration and does this satisfy, in any way, the desire for more local control?

One immediate and important advantage which is available for any regional Ministry, such as St Andrew's House, is in terms of the size of the area to be covered. Officials in such sections as housing and local government know the thirty-one County Clerks as individuals, the men in the Department of Education and the Inspectors have a definite picture of the conditions and atmosphere in every education authority, while the Department of Agriculture can describe the practices on certain individual farms. It is a help in this respect that the majority of the administrative class civil servants (precise figures are not available) are Scotsmen educated at Scottish schools and universities.

There was, however, till very recently, no general appreciation in St Andrew's House (or in Whitehall) of the need to collect more information than personal acquaintance and the actual process of administration provided. In the case of some functions it would clearly be superfluous to repeat or supplement work already done at a United Kingdom level. Thus the sections of the Home and Health Department which deal with the police and with criminal justice carry out little or no research on police techniques or on criminology but participate in the financing and oversight of the Home Office studies of these questions.

On economic development, there has since 1945 been an annual White Paper on Industry and Employment in Scotland and a biannual Digest of Scottish Statistics. Yet before 1962 there were no economists in St Andrew's House and no individual, group or department charged with examining the Scottish economy or preparing proposals to put to the Ministers.

When the area's economic imbalance had persisted for so long that it was clearly a serious problem, the work of diagnosis and prescription had to be carried out by a private body, albeit with considerable government assistance, the Scottish Council for Development and Industry. It appointed a committee under Mr (now Sir) J. N. Toothill which produced a major report. One of its proposals was that those sections of the Home and Health Departments which dealt with roads, electricity, local government, housing and town planning should be collected into a single unit. This was done in June 1962 and the Scottish Development Department was created. Within it a Development Group was formed to assemble information, and

Administration Devolution in Scotland

U.K. Ministers (Most with Regional Offices and Scottish Controllers)	Inter-departmental Committees	Secretary of State for Scotland Minister of State, 3 Under-secretaries (Lord Advocate and Solicitor-General backed by their own staffs) Four Departments in St Andrew's House (with examples of subordinate bodies)
1. Labour		
2. Transport (Railways, Steamers)	1. Distribution of Industry Panel	1. Development Department
3. Board of Trade (including Regional Development)	2. Scottish Development Board	North of Scotland Hydro Board
4. Defence (incorporating the former War Office, Admiralty and Air Ministry)	3. Building Committees (further *ad hoc* Committees)	South of Scotland Electricity Board Advisory Committees on Water Housing, Building and Civil Engineering
5. Public Buildings and Works		
6. Aviation		2. Home and Health Department
Advisory Council for Scotland		5 Regional Hospital Boards
7. Fuel and Power		25 Executive Councils (G.P.s)
Scottish Gas Board		5 Joint Ophthalmic Service Committees
Scottish Division N.C.B.		Mental Welfare Commission
8. Pensions and Insurance		4 Medical Education Committees
9. National Assistance Board		Scottish Health Service Council (advisory)
10. Post Office		Advisory Council on Child Care
11. Inland Revenue		Scottish Police Council
12. Customs and Excise		Scottish Central Probation Council

3. Agricultural and Fisheries Department
   11 Agricultural Executive Committees
   8 Agricultural Research Institutions
   3 Agricultural Colleges
4. Education Department
   Advisory Council on Education
   National Commission for Teacher
     Training
   Royal Scottish Museum

Scottish Authorities, Commissions, etc.

Crofters' Commission
Highland Development Board
Countryside Commission
Red Deer Commission
   (All appointed by Secretary of State)
Scottish Board for Industry
   (appointed by Chancellor of
   Exchequer)

U.K. Authorities, Commissions, etc.	
A. Forestry Commission (Scottish Commission)	All under Secretary of State for their Scottish activities
B. Herring Industry Board	
C. White Fish Authority	
D. Crown Lands Commission	
E. Nature Conservancy (under Privy Council)	
F. Council of Industrial Design (Board of Trade)	
G. University Grants Commission (Treasury)	
H. Land Commission (Ministry of Land and Natural Resources)	

to prepare and supervise the execution of economic plans for Central Scotland and later for the Highlands and the Borders. The Development Group does not contain an economic unit similar to the Economic Section of the Treasury, but some of the administrators are trained as economists and are available to advise on any specifically economic problems. There is also a sociologist who is employed in analysing any information included in the 1961 census which might prove useful to the Group and eleven officers who deal generally with land use planning and demographic questions. The effectiveness of the Development Group is revealed by the degree to which the White Paper on Central Scotland (Cmnd. 2188) was in advance of the plan released at the same time for North-East England where there was no regional administration to undertake the preparation.

The Department of Agriculture and Fisheries for Scotland aids or maintains eight agricultural research institutions, but these are entirely concerned with husbandry, animal nutrition, plant breeding, cattle diseases, dairy problems, soil research and so on. There are probably no specifically Scottish agricultural problems (no necessity to work on Highland as distinct from marginal agriculture) and it would be reasonable to regard these institutions as that part of the British effort in agricultural research which happens to be located in Scotland.

There are in the Department seven agricultural economists whose primary task is to collect statistics on farm output, employment and income, to produce a biannual return and provide the foundation on which the annual price review is based. This team also studies the effects of government policies and scientific advances on agriculture and, with the cooperation of the three agricultural colleges, has built up a fair stock of material, some of which is published annually in *Scottish Agricultural Economics*. Together with the experience of the two hundred or more inspectors employed by the Department, this Department is well equipped to advise and comment on any problems of policy submitted to them.

For education, housing and those aspects of the health services that are conducted by the local authorities, the shortage of information is more marked. The Scottish Education Department till recently only assembled the information which arose in the course of its work. When the Robbins Committee reported in late 1963, the figures of anticipated demand for university places (compiled not by the Ministry of Education in Whitehall, which was also backward in this respect, but by Professor C. A. Moser and a research team which included officials from the departments concerned) caused such surprise that there was a slight change of attitude and the Department now has the part-time services of one statistician. On matters like the number of schools in current use which were built before 1900 or before 1939 or the degree of overcrowding, no precise or even rough answers can be given. The Department sometimes asks the local authorities to report on these points but they are usually too busy running their services to collect the facts. There are some eighty inspectors who form a reservoir of opinion and information on which the senior officials can draw and they furnish an annual (unpublished) report on the work of each local education authority. When the Scottish Office produced its equivalent of the Crowther Report (the Brunton Report), as in England, it was necessary for the committee to compile the necessary data before it could consider the problem. However, once the need for research is appreciated, the task of such a Department dealing with five million people is more manageable than that facing a Whitehall Ministry and it is therefore possible to do a more thorough job and to keep a personal check on the accuracy of the information.

The same trends are noticeable in housing. At the time of the 1961 Census it was reported that there were 412,853 houses lacking a fixed bath, but there was no information as to how many were slums and how many could be improved at a reasonable cost. Then, as research became fashionable in government, St Andrew's House followed suit. An Advisory Council was reconstituted for Housing and it commissioned a series of reports, the one entitled *Scotland's Older Houses* (the Cullingworth Report) being a most thorough survey which filled all these gaps. A series of further reports covered the subjects of *Housing Management in Scotland* and *Allocating Council Houses*.

In health and welfare services, there was the same difficulty: the total need for home helps and meals-on-wheels was not estimated because the local authorities were not able to supply the information. The aspects of the Health Service dealt with by the Scottish Office were not systematically studied till 1965 when an Operational Research Unit was established in St Andrew's House, policy having been based hitherto principally on the mortality figures provided by the Registrar General for Scotland.

Thus the record of the Scottish Office shows that, though a regional ministry is closer to the local authorities in terms of personal contacts and though it can investigate problems which are entirely relevant to the needs of the area it covers, this is not done till operational research becomes acceptable to the entire civil service; that is, till Whitehall moves from a regulatory to an interventionist view of its own role. When this happens a Ministry organized on the lines of the Scottish Office has an overall view of one region and a loyalty to and continuing interest in that region which permits and encourages the best kind of work in this field.

Turning to the criterion of whether a regional ministry provides better co-ordination, a simpler form of administrative control, more rapid action and the adaptation of national policies to the needs of the region, it is hard to penetrate official secrecy about the process of administration in order to find an answer. The only method available is to consider the evidence put before the Select Committee on Estimates when it studied a single subject and compared the methods of administration of the Whitehall Department with the equivalent section of the Scottish Office.

In the case of trunk roads, in 1956 responsibility was transferred from the Ministry of Transport to the Secretary of State for Scotland. Building trunk roads is slow throughout the United Kingdom largely because of the procedure laid down by the Trunk Roads Act 1946 and the Special Roads Act 1949, the vast majority of the time being taken in the planning, acquisition of powers and of land and in obtaining tenders. Thus the preparatory stages for the M.1 motorway took eight years while the actual construction of the road was then completed in a further twenty months. To explain this process to the Select Committee on Estimates, the County Surveyor of the West Riding of Yorkshire submitted a table of the thirty-one separate steps or stages that have to be carried through before work can start on improving or building a trunk road. Cut to the minimum, these amount to:

1. The need for a new or improved road has to be accepted by the ministry.
2. They ask the local authority to draw a line for the road.
3. If this seems satisfactory, a Trunk Road Order is published.
4. There is a three-month delay to permit objections. If these cannot be settled,
5. A public inquiry is held, and a report submitted.
6. Report accepted or rejected by the Secretary of State. If the former,
7. Trunk Road Order made and the schedule for land required drawn up.
8. If the owners of the land refuse to sell, a compulsory purchase order is made. If there are objections, there must be a public inquiry and report.

9. When land is acquired, the local authority is asked to call for tenders.

10. One tender is accepted and work can then begin.

In Scotland, the fact that there is no Divisional Road Engineer but just a Chief Road Engineer and also that there is no division between the Chief Valuer and District Valuer means that two of the least difficult of the thirty-one steps can be cut out. But the other twenty-nine (all ten of the condensed version given above) remain, and the procedure on Trunk Road Orders and Compulsory Purchase Orders may well take longer, as in Scotland the inquiries are not given to an Inspector but to an experienced member of the Scottish bar. This involves finding an advocate with time to spare for what is at that level very poorly paid work, and waiting for him to hear evidence, adjust all statements of fact with the objecting parties and then frame a final report. This has been known to take nine months or a year. As a result each section of a trunk road takes two to three years to authorize and about two years to construct if there are no snags or persistent objectors, while if these occur the time can be stretched out almost indefinitely (as happened with the stretch of the A80 past Denny and Cumbernauld which took from 1956 to 1965), and the entire process in Scotland takes quite as long as in England.

While trunk roads (or principal roads, as they are now called) are the direct responsibility of the Scottish Office, the remaining roads are under the control of the cities, counties and large burghs, which receive grants from the Scottish Office for road building and maintenance and have to submit all their plans to St Andrew's House for approval. The procedure is simpler than that for principal roads, the main limiting factor being finance, but other questions which arise are the method of control, the selection of suitable schemes, and their integration with principal roads, as well as with industrial and urban development.

In Scotland, the Chief Road Engineer combines the responsibilities of a Divisonal Road Engineer in England with those of the Highways Engineering Staff in Whitehall, thus cutting out one step in the ladder of command. Also there is no Area Finance Officer, as the Finance Division of the Scottish Development Department combines the duties of an A.F.O. with those of the Finance Division of the U.K. Ministry, thus eliminating the need for this double check. The local authorities prepare their schemes and submit them directly to the Chief Road Engineer. For those costing under £10,000 a general grant is made. Schemes of over £10,000 have to be worked out in detail and are re-examined by the C.R.E.'s staff and then put on the list from which a few (about a quarter in practice) are selected for approval. Quarterly reports have to be submitted on all such projects. Plans for road construction costing over £100,000 have to be submitted by the Scottish Office to the Treasury.

The Estimates Committee in 1961–2 endorsed the view of the Association of County Councils for Scotland that since St Andrew's House took over trunk roads 'there has been a trend for expansion in the administrative field which on occasion tends to increase complexity and impede progress in the technical field by decreasing the freedom and authority which the Chief Road Engineer in his former role as Divisional Road Engineer previously enjoyed'. This retarded road schemes and 'the result has proved to be very frustrating and is the cause of considerable uneasiness'. Mr A. Smith of Lanark County Council enlarged on this, saying that 'possibly there is a stronger financial control in the ... Department now than there was a few years ago, and perhaps this is the reason for the delay in schemes which by and large have been approved by the engineers' side'.

Comparing the practices of the Ministry of Transport with those of the Scottish Office, in England schemes costing under

£25,000 were accepted without detailed examination while in Scotland the figure was £10,000. The official in charge said 'I am quite prepared to believe we are now getting details of schemes which ten or fifteen years before, or even before the war, did not come near the central engineering departments.' In Scotland quarterly reports had to be submitted for all road works costing over £10,000, while in England this was only required if the figure was over £100,000. (The Secretary of State for Scotland and the Minister of Transport in 1963 'accepted in principle' the recommendation of the Estimates Committee that details need not be submitted for schemes costing under £50,000 but whether this has been put into practice is not known.)

An example of the kind of difficulty that can arise occurred over the Clyde Tunnels. Powers to build the tunnels were granted in 1948 but it was not till 1954 that the Ministry of Transport agreed to provide a grant and work began. By 1957 the Scottish Office was in control and decreed that there was not enough money for direct approach roads to be built and Glasgow Corporation began to build more limited links with the existing roads. Then traffic needs were reassessed and the Scottish Office decided that these links would be inadequate and direct approaches were restored. This meant knocking down a wall that had already been built for the modified scheme involving a waste of some £80,000. The Estimates Committee blamed the fact that planning was divided between the Scottish Home and Health Departments and said that there had not been adequate liaison between them and the Corporation of Glasgow.

In general, the Estimates Committee concluded that 'detailed controls suitable to the expenditure of comparatively small sums on classified roads are still being applied to a larger road programme for which a different system of control could be more effective', and left the general impression that

in Scotland this tendency was, on the whole, more evident
than in the Ministry of Transport.

On the question of relevance to local needs, 'the Sub-
Committee could obtain no evidence as to the existence of a
national plan for classified roads', and the failure to link classified road authorizations with trunk road building and with
industrial and urban development was commented on without
distinguishing between the performance north and south of the
Border.

The building of schools was also examined by the Estimates
Committee and the procedure and effectiveness of the Scottish
Education Department was compared directly with that of the
Ministry of Education. The procedure for authorizing a new
building costing over £50,000 consists of a series of stages,
those that are obligatory (as opposed to informal consultations
between local authority officials, H.M. Inspectors of Schools
and the Department's architects) being:

1. The education authority seeks approval in principal to
the erection of a new school by applying on Form S.B.1 to the
Scottish Education Department through the H.M. Inspector
for the district.

2. The proposal is considered by the Department and is
approved (with or without amendment) or rejected. If approved, the common cost limit for the project is set.

3. Proposals for the site are submitted on Form S.B.2:
these are likewise considered and approved or rejected.

4. Plans and estimated costs are submitted on Form S.B.4.

5. These are considered by the Department and approved
with or without alteration.

6. Permission to borrow is requested on Form S.B.5.

7. Provided approved costs (see 5) are not exceeded, the
authority may invite tenders and let the contract, merely
reporting details on Form S.B.6.

For primary schools, this procedure can take up to two years, while for secondary schools there are considerable variations, the time span being usually three to five years. In addition to the various scrutinies by the architects and inspectors of the Scottish Education Department, plans for new schools have to be sent round the other departments to check the use of land, possible changes in population and transport facilities.

Apart from the political decision as to how much money should be invested in new or modernized schools, the local authorities and their Directors of Education were very critical of this system before it was revised in 1966. They argued that there was too much control and unnecessary delays especially at what is now the S.B.4 stage which often took nine months or a year. Then plans might be sent back with demands for minor economies leading to a further delay of possibly over a year which, with rising labour costs, could (and had on quoted occasions) increased the cost by more than the amount saved by the economies. They held that it would be far quicker and cause less friction if the Director of Education and the Department's Inspector saw the plans and simply submitted a report that all regulations had been observed. The local authorities were in fact spending their own money; they had every interest in economy and if the school included special facilities it was because local circumstances required them. The result of all these criticisms was that one stage inspection was cut out, for projects costing £50,000 or less neither schedules of accommodation nor plans were required, and for minor works costing less than £5,000 (unless the project involved nursery classes or houses) only permission to borrow was required.

The Scottish Education Department was for some time handicapped because it had only four architects employed on the task of revision and there were consequent delays in St Andrew's House, but the Department always insisted that some of the smaller and weaker authorities required this aid (rather than supervision) and that it was necessary to ensure good value for public money. Many educational features and possible extravagances had to be questioned and the whole procedure was admittedly based on a political decision that marginal economies were more important than very rapid action.

In 1961, the Estimates Committee said they were 'not satisfied that the system of giving notice of major works programmes in Scotland is as well arranged as it is in England'. They criticized over-rigid controls, the fixing of cost in relation to area rather than per pupil ('leads to less freedom and incentive for the arhictect and tends to more uniformity in design'), and concluded that 'the Scottish procedure for approval compares very unfavourably with that now employed by the Ministry of Education'. After this blast, there were a number of changes, those mentioned on the previous page cutting down the number of obligatory references to St Andrew's House by one. In addition, common cost limits were determined as in England in relation to the number of pupils on the roll.

In 1961–2 the Estimates Committee investigated the dental services and compared procedures and costs in England and in Scotland. The results were somewhat mixed as the final report recommended that the Scottish Dental Estimates Board was uneconomic and should be amalgamated with the English Board while commending the Scottish Regional Dental Officers. The latter saw 1,500 cases a year as opposed to under 1,000 in England and also supervised the local authorities' dental services. The primary one of these is the school dental service and here the work was much less intensively done in Scotland than in England, though in both cases the number of children examined by each dentist had fallen off sharply in the last ten years. But at least the Scottish Home and Health Department was alarmed by the position and had been making investigations. The Estimates Committee thought 'it may well be asked why the Ministries have been so slow in taking effective measures to improve the service and also why it is that the efforts to deal with the situation recently appear to be so much more considerable in Scotland than in England and Wales'. The Scottish system whereby the school dental services come under the Department of Health rather than the Department of Education and are supervised by the Regional Dental Officers was commended despite the poorer ratio of children examined per dentist north of the Border.

In general all this investigation suggested was that, while a regional service could take more time and care over problems, it might cost more, as the Dental Estimates Board in Scotland was taking 2·45 per cent of fees for running expenses as opposed to only 1·49 per cent in England and Wales.

No comparative material exists on slum clearance but as it is a problem which bulks large in Scottish administration, certain points are worth noticing. The basic factors are political, but as an administrative problem the time taken to authorize slum clearance schemes depends on procedures which are accepted practice in the Civil Service both in Whitehall and in St Andrew's House. Under the Housing Acts local authorities can take action against slums in one of three main ways:

(a) they can require owners of individual properties to repair them;

(b) if the houses cannot be repaired at reasonable expense the local authorities may make closing or demolition orders for individual unfit houses;

(c) local authorities may go further and designate a 'clearance area' and demolish all the houses within that area.

Relatively little use has been made of the last method, partly because it is much easier to proceed piecemeal against individual unfit houses and partly because the major authorities prefer comprehensive redevelopment under the Planning Acts. But, as an example of a clearance scheme where the procedure worked as rapidly as could be expected, the Burgh of Hamilton promoted a number of linked clearance areas, and made Compulsory Purchase Orders in October 1961. All the stages, notification and paper work were completed, the land and buildings acquired, and all the areas cleared for redevelopment by December 1964, so that the whole business, from first conception to the complete clearance of the sites, took just over three years. In this case all objections were settled privately by negotiation between the local authority and the individual owners so that no public inquiry was needed. A more normal timetable was that illustrated by the scheme for the Stockbridge area of Edinburgh. The City's sanitary authorities inspected the houses and decided to take action in 1961. A clearance resolution was passed by the Corporation in March 1962 and in August four Compulsory Purchase Orders were published. There were eighteen objections and a public inquiry was ordered and held in July 1963. The Secretary of State received the report in early 1964 and confirmed the Purchase Orders. Then the occupiers had to be offered alternative accommodation, the premises valued, each owner located, compensated, and the title conveyed to the local authority. Only in 1965 did demolition begin, so the legal processes even after the confirmation of the Compulsory Purchase Orders can take many months or even years.

None of these stages can be cut short unless a definite decision is taken to speed up the processes of public inquiry or of acquisition and compensation which are laid down as standard practice by Parliament or by Whitehall. In the first case the present procedure, which involves the finding of an advocate with time to spare, the arranging of a suitable date for an inquiry, the interchange of objections and answers to objections, the adjustment of findings of fact and possible delays in the drafting of the report, could be shortened without any significant loss to the rights of the citizen. This is probably true in the procedure for all public inquiries but is especially so where the property concerned is by definition unfit for human habitation and in itself worthless.

In the particular circumstances of Scotland, even after the issue of compulsory purchase has been settled, considerable delays can occur before the local authority obtains a valid title to the land, because of the way in which the ownership of the characteristic blocks of flats or 'tenements' has been broken up. A single tenement can be owned by a large number of different people, some of whom may be difficult to trace perhaps because they have deliberately absconded to escape their obligations to repair ruinous property. Again some of the houses in a tenement may have been sold off for owner-occupation very cheaply without a proper legal title having been given. This could have happened several times over with even one house so that the true legal ownership is obscure. In these circumstances a local authority could have great difficulty in tracing the legal owners in order both to serve the necessary statutory notices upon them and to gain possession of a valid legal title themselves.

To meet this situation the Scottish civil servants devised a simplified procedure which was included in the Housing and Town Development (Scotland) Act of 1957. Under Section 22, when a Compulsory Purchase Order has been confirmed, the recording of the order in the Register of Sasines in Edinburgh will serve as a 'block' notice, so saving the local authority the time and trouble of serving individual notices on all the persons concerned. The local authority may then, simply by declaring notice of their intention, and recording it in the Register of Sasines, obtain valid, legal ownership of the property, which they can then clear and redevelop or sell to a developer as they wish. The detailed procedure for settling the compensation with any owner who may appear and make a claim is left over to be completed at leisure.

In the Housing (Scotland) Act of 1962, the officials introduced several improvements in the procedure for dealing with individual unfit houses. Previously, before the local authority could make an order to close or demolish they had to allow the owner of the property a chance to give an undertaking to repair it and make it fit for habitation. This had occurred only in very rare cases and Section 21 of the 1962 Act cut out the prelimiary notice and enabled the local authority to make a demolition order at once which could be suspended if an owner came forward with an undertaking to renovate. Also local authorities had had the power to demolish unfit houses and recover their expenses from the owners. But since the owners of the older tenements are often hard to find, Sections 22 and 23 of the Act gave the authorities the right simply to acquire the sites of demolished houses in order to cover their expenses or to make a 'charging order' on the land which would give the authority a prior claim on any income which might later arise from it.

To sum up these examples, the Scottish Office tends to follow very closely the administrative patterns laid down in Whitehall. Perhaps because it has, on the whole, smaller and weaker local authorities to deal with, perhaps because of the more inflexible aspects of the Scottish character, there is no evidence of any propensity to reduce or simplify the methods of supervision unless this is also being done by the equivalent department in Whitehall. On the other hand, there is evidence that a regional administration dealing with local peculiarities, such as the complicated legal tenure of Scottish tenements, can make minor but useful improvements on its own initiative.

Finally, there is the test of whether this type of administrative organization covering most domestic services run by Scotsmen in Scotland, does remove the grievance about remote London-based government. The answer is clearly in the negative. Even before this was demonstrated for all to see by the rise of the Scottish National Party (S.N.P.) the division of responsibility between U.K. Ministries and the Scottish Office was often obscure in fact and made worse by the cloak of secrecy which shrouds most of British government. The *Report of the Royal Commission on Scottish Affairs, 1952-1954* (Cmnd. 9212) frequently observed that many electors in Scotland have no idea of the actual extent of administrative devolution. S.N.P. orators can claim, without arousing any disbelief, that Scotland on all questions is ruled from Whitehall and on one occasion this was asserted in a village meeting where the permanent secretary of one of the St Andrew's House departments was actually a resident and present at the meeting. Even for those informed about the processes of government, the precise division of responsibility for industrial development between the D.E.A. (which includes regional planning), the Board of Trade (which grants I.D.C.s) and the Scottish Development Department is not clear. After the 1954 Royal Commission, the Veterinary Service was supposed to be transferred to the Scottish Office but though its members in Scotland come under the Secretary of State, they are part of a unified service run by the Minister for Agriculture. In part this obscurity has been encouraged by the description of the Secretary of State as 'Scotland's Minister' and the assumption that 'although he has no direct responsibility for the branches of the national administration entrusted to U.K. . . . Ministers, he is vitally and inescapably interested in the application to Scotland of the policies of the Government in these fields'. This has a certain prestige value but it only confuses citizens when 'Scotland's Minister' is pressed on a Scottish point and insists that the responsibility does not lie with him but with the appropriate U.K. Minister.

The final proof of the inadequacy of administrative devolution in satisfying the desire for more local control and participation has been that it is precisely where this process has gone furthest, in Scotland, that the rejection of the present system of local and central government has gone furthest, the evidence being both the voting record and propaganda of the S.N.P.

Since the Scottish civil servants are recognized to be able and industrious, it is most important to establish why they are so little known or appreciated in the country which they administer. One reason is that it is accepted doctrine that civil servants in the Scottish Office do not get out of line in either policy or administrative procedures with their opposite numbers in the English departments. When it is trying to enforce economies, the Treasury is fond of comparing costs of similar operations conducted by the English Ministries and by the Scottish Office. The Estimates Committee, as has been observed, tends to dwell on any differences it can detect and ask if one practice is preferable to the other. The salient point is that Ministers are members of a single Cabinet and subject to attack in the House of Commons. If M.P.s discover that methods or priorities are different in Scotland they are almost certain to ask why the one or other country is favoured or penalized, developed or retarded as compared with the other. Scotland, by virtue of its particular industrial and social history, requires more government aid for industry, a greater effort in slum clearance, and costs more in terms of social security. Thus, whether a Labour or a Conservative Government is in power, Scottish administrators are constantly in danger of creating dangerous precedents for their English counterparts. They have had their successes. Housing subsidies, for instance, are higher in Scotland than in England and so are some agricultural subsidies, but Ministers are very conscious of the need for consistency in their policy at a national level and are careful to avoid commitments in Scotland that might have wider repercussions. The result is that at an official level it is an accepted contention that no Scottish civil servant makes a proposal without having first cleared it with Whitehall. As Sir John Winnifrith, the Permanent Secretary at the Ministry of Agriculture, told the Select Committee on Agriculture in 1967: 'If ever we fall down on that [the convention about consultation], it is purely by something going wrong through human failure. Our working rule is that all our policy has to be cleared between the two Departments.'

Financial arrangements have the same effect. The expenditure for the Scottish Office is not voted as a single sum leaving Scottish Ministers free to move money from roads to schools or to industrial development as they feel the priorities require. The investment in school building is worked out as part of a national policy on this subject, and the money for hospitals is negotiated between the English and Scottish Departments of Health acting together and the Treasury. Thus there are financial, administrative and heavy political pressures brought to bear on St Andrew's House to make it operate in a manner and according to priorities which are as close as possible to those of Whitehall. It is scarcely surprising that as a result few can distinguish between Scottish and English patterns of action. Comprehensive schools are taken up simultaneously, north and south of the Border, so is regional development and a policy for preserving the countryside. The great pride of the civil service is not that it has developed special methods or a different emphasis in Scotland, but rather that no gap can be found between Edinburgh and London methods so that no politically awkward questions can be raised.

The lessons for the purpose of this investigation are that no amount of regional *administrative* devolution can make people feel they have more local control. Small adaptations of administrative practice can be made (as over tenement clearance) but the pressure for uniformity created by one political master puts all the emphasis on uniformity of practice. The grievance about 'remote government' is not racial or spatial, it arises despite the fact that the decisions are not taken by Englishmen in London. It arises because there is no political control in

Scotland, no democratically elected body in Scotland to which the regional civil servants could be responsible. If this happened, there would be a positive incentive to be different, to take local needs into consideration rather than to struggle to be the same. Regional administration has great potential virtues but they will not be realized till political control of these functions is transferred to a separate, independently elected body in each region.

The Greater London Council

There is one further current experiment in regionalism from which something might be learned and that is the brief experience of the Greater London Council (G.L.C.) formed in 1963. Unlike the planning councils, which are advisory bodies, and the Scottish Office, which is a regional executive ministry, the G.L.C. is elected and was devised to cover what is a conurbation but in numerical terms might be classed as a region, Greater London.

The history of this experiment really dates from 1899 when the London County Council was established, to govern four out of the five million people living in the metropolis. By 1961, Greater London numbered eight million, of whom only three million lived in the L.C.C. area. The rest came under the jurisdiction of six county councils, three county borough councils, eighty-five borough, metropolitan borough and urban district councils, and the Common Council of the City. With this multiplicity of authorities, no single local authority was responsible for traffic management or for deciding how many houses were needed or for building new housing schemes and carrying out overspill projects. Yet London is in many ways a single entity requiring a single directing body both for reasons of efficiency and to reflect civic pride.

A Royal Commission under Sir Edwin Herbert was appointed in 1957 and considered several possible solutions. They rejected the idea that the overall needs of London should be met by direct action from Whitehall (perhaps a Ministry for London affairs), not on the grounds that it would be inefficient or impractical but because it would mean the end of responsible elected self-government in the capital. The Commission also looked at the possible solution of creating *ad hoc* bodies for each of the major services but gave this proposal up because so many of the essential functions interlock and cannot be managed in isolation. A third possibility consisted of joint boards created by the existing local councils, but this was put aside as adding to the complexity of administration without providing adequate control by elected representatives.

The London Government Bill introduced in late 1962 therefore created the Greater London Council with the principal task of watching over the whole planning and development of the capital. The G.L.C. was allocated the strategic tasks of planning, regulating traffic, the siting, building and maintaining of houses, major road-building and overspill programmes. It also supervised main drainage, ambulance and fire services and refuse disposal. A new feature of the G.L.C. was the specific power to create a high level Research and Intelligence Unit.

As a second tier, thirty-two borough councils were formed (the Royal Commission had recommended fifty-two) which were to undertake most of the work of local government and have all powers apart from those just listed. It followed that personal services to help the sick, the aged, those physically or mentally handicapped, the needs of children and the homeless were all allocated to the boroughs which, with an average population of 250,000, were held to be capable of hiring adequate staff and maintaining a proper service. The boroughs also had the major responsibility for housing in their areas and for sewage and were given the normal powers of sanitary authorities under the Public Health Acts. Parks which were not of interest to the whole metropolis (such as Hampstead Heath) were assigned to the boroughs and they were also the primary authorities for food and drugs.

The Government departed from the recommendations of the Royal Commission for sharing education between the G.L.C. and the boroughs. The outer twenty boroughs were given the entire responsibility for education while in the area which had formerly come under the L.C.C., now referred to as Inner London, a single Inner London Education Authority was constituted, ostensibly as an offshoot of the G.L.C. but in reality with a large measure of independence.

While education was given this special treatment, some other functions were divided between the two tiers, the main examples being planning (where the details and the powers to allocate land for different uses lay with the boroughs while 'overall strategy' was left to the G.L.C.), roads and housing. It was also evident that there would have to be some co-operation among the outer London boroughs and between them and the I.L.E.A. in the provision of some specialized aspects of further education, in the use of approved and special schools and in the running of the children's service.

The G.L.C. was composed of 100 councillors, to be elected at triennial elections, and 16 aldermen, the first election being held in April 1964. This was won by the Labour Party but there was a dramatic reversal when the Conservatives virtually swept the board in the elections of 1967. The staff was largely recruited from the former L.C.C., the Metropolitan boroughs and the other local authorities that were replaced by this new structure.

Now in 1968 it is possible to make some comments on the way in which this form of regional government, dealing with a population greater than that of several European countries, has operated; it is possible to consider whether it might serve as a model for a reformed system of local government and whether a G.L.C. type structure would be suitable for the large regional councils.

In terms of population and resources, the G.L.C. would be better off than any regions other than the South-East and the question is how far it has been able to make use of its opportunities. On the one hand, certain major projects have been contemplated or started which would have been impossible without an authority of the size of the G.L.C. A Development Plan is being prepared for the whole area, a traffic scheme, including a motorway box around Central London (at a cost of £400 million) has been drawn up, overspill housing schemes are in progress, a new £9 million refuse disposal unit is the first of its kind in Britain and there have been ambitious amenity projects such as the Lea Valley Regional Park. The boroughs, for their part, have considerable resources at their disposal and it is conceded that standards have improved, particularly in welfare services and in primary and secondary education in the outer boroughs.

On the other hand, there have been inadequacies and disputes arising in part from the original Act, in part from the division of responsibilities between the G.L.C. and the boroughs, but also from the way in which the creation of a regional unit was treated in so many respects as if it were just a matter of enlarging an existing local authority. Also the boundaries of the G.L.C. omitted parts of the South-West built-up area which has caused some problems, while the share of joint responsibilities in planning, housing, highways and traffic was often unclear and even when it was clear, was not always sensible.

In the case of planning, not all the boroughs have been able to appoint fully qualified officers. Yet the control of the allocation of land for the various purposes of development lies with the boroughs and this leaves Westminster and a number of other boroughs with the power to prevent any comprehensive treatment of the vital central area of London. The G.L.C. can designate 'areas of special interest' and withdraw them from the control of the boroughs, but this does not give the G.L.C. the overall capacity to plan for the area. As a result, there is considerable tension between the boroughs and the G.L.C. and instead of the upper-tier authority having the final decision in disputed matters, appeals go to the Ministry of Housing and Local Government, thus introducing a third authority and leading to prolonged delays.

The new Highways and Transportation Department of the G.L.C. is competent and well-staffed, though its engineers are more interested in traffic movement than in the effect of motorways on amenities or local community linkages. The main difficulty is that the Act divided responsibility, allocating trunk roads to the Ministry of Transport, 550 miles of metropolitan roads to the G.L.C. (with planning powers for 220 feet on each side of these roads) and the remaining roads to the boroughs. To complicate traffic matters even further, there is the London Passenger Transport Board, whose separate executive is to come under G.L.C. control, and the Metropolitan Police who also have powers to supervise traffic control and to license taxis. A Traffic Commissioner at the Ministry licenses buses and fixes routes and stopping places, and so no single authority watches over parking or the total regulation of driving, pedestrian ways and road safety. It is not surprising that there is constant confusion and conflict over highway and traffic matters and the G.L.C. in 1968 was contemplating trading 150,000 of its stock of 250,000 houses in return for the boroughs surrendering all traffic control and roads. This would probably be a better distribution of housing though the G.L.C. argues that it must retain a considerable stock of accommodation in order to have places for people displaced by its redevelopment plans, while the boroughs are not happy at the existence of two systems of house management and two rent schemes side by side.

The same sort of confusion exists over parks, some being under the Crown (and therefore run by the Ministry of Works) while large open areas are G.L.C. supervised and small parks are managed by the boroughs. In education, it is not altogether satisfactory that the Inner London Education Authority also manages the School Medical Service which is thus cut off from the other welfare services run by the boroughs. On the other hand, in terms of education alone, the I.L.E.A. shows up very well and many of the neighbouring outer boroughs rely on it in part for extra places in secondary education and for special schools. (There are 94 special schools in the I.L.E.A. area and only 60 in the outer boroughs though their population is twice as large.) The chief defect of the outer boroughs in this sphere is in further education where the staff and expertise are not adequate.

Apart from these problems over functions, the main weakness of the new London government is the way in which the legislation, internal structures and staff attitudes which had grown up around the counties and county boroughs were simply reproduced on a larger scale. The same committee structure and detailed staff regulations were enforced by statute. On this question the Greater London Group of the London School of Economics, in its study *The Lessons of the London Government Reforms*, quotes the London Boroughs Association's evidence to the Seebohm Committee:

Parliament's efforts hitherto in the direction of governing the internal organization of local authorities have been piecemeal and on each occasion directed to limited objectives. The result is a patchwork quilt of statutory requirements which lacks logic, encourages excessive compartmentalism, and severely restricts the scope for local authorities to experiment with new forms of committee and staff structures.

Thus, for example, London Boroughs are required to appoint Health, Children's, Welfare and even, in some cases, Allotments Committees (though Welfare may be combined with some other Committee with the Minister's consent) and Outer London Boroughs must appoint Education Committees. Oddly enough, although housing is one of the most important services, there is no statutory provision requiring the appointment of a Housing Committee. Nor are London Boroughs required to appoint Finance Committees (though County Councils are required to do so).

The patchwork quilt requires London Boroughs to appoint a clerk, a treasurer, a medical officer of health, a surveyor, a children's officer, an architect (by 1968) and, in the case of Outer London Boroughs, a chief education officer. They are not, however, required to appoint a planning officer, housing manager, librarian or welfare officer. Statute spells out in some detail the duties of some of these officers, such as the medical officer of health and the children's officer; in the case of some of the other officers, such as the clerk and the surveyor, the statutory duties are very limited in comparison with the functions they in fact perform: in the case of the architect the statute merely provides that one must be appointed but assigns no duties to the post. Another vagary allows the authorities, if so minded, to spend unlimited sums of money, without any report from the treasurer. Anomalies of this nature abound.

When the Maud Committee on Management condemned many of these practices, the G.L.C. set up a Special Committee on Procedure. It recommended the amalgamation of the Finance, Supplies and Establishment Committees into a single body and the union of the Fire Brigade and Ambulance Committees, but otherwise concluded that all was well. No directing board or cabinet was created and the committee structure was left largely intact because it was thought that otherwise there would be nothing for rank and file elected councillors to do.

In some ways the most serious deficiency on the part of the Herbert Commission was the lack of attention paid to staff problems. The G.L.C. is, for some purposes, a regional government, yet its officials came from town halls and have retained their former habits of mind, particularly in their deep departmental loyalties. Thus the project for a new town, Thamesmead, tended to fall between departmental stools. The planners employed were mainly of the 1947 Town and Country Planning Act vintage and did not appreciate strategic planning, their first attempt at a development plan being virtually turned down by the Ministry. Meanwhile the Research and Intelligence Unit, which had been such a good idea, complained that no one knew how to use its expertise, how to understand the significance of population projections (showing an actual fall in Central London) or how to put capital expenditure programmes together to produce a single reliable forecast of costs. Lastly, there is little evidence that London's problems or interests were or are being considered in the light of the South-East Region and its overall requirements.

Judged in terms of popular participation, the standard of G.L.C. councillors has been high, and the turnout in the elections of 1964 was some eight per cent more than in the previous county or L.C.C. elections, while the borough turnout rose between eight per cent and eighteen per cent, the big increase being in the outer boroughs. In large part, however, this was due to the activity of the national parties who treated the elections as a commentary on the record of the national government. Surveys showed that the public knew little about the G.L.C. or its work and while 50 per cent could name their M.P., only two per cent could name a councillor. Here again some of the blame lies in the use of the committee system and the restricted powers of the G.L.C. so that no one emerged as 'the Prime Minister of London'. Even if the Chairman of the G.L.C. had aspired to that position, there was not enough freedom from Whitehall control to make a real impact and thus to arouse keen popular interest.

It seems clear that as a unit for administration the province or planning region is most suitable, and London government has a narrower vision because it is restricted to a large part of a single conurbation. It is also clear that appointed advisory boards lack the independent authority to stand up to the central government or to cut across the traditionally vertical organization of the Whitehall departments. They are also unable to impose their wishes on elected local councils. A horizontally organized department such as the Scottish Office has many advantages but it cannot experiment, it cannot transfer resources from one area of activity to another and it cannot establish a separate order of priorities because it is subject to the same political control being directed by the single Cabinet and responsible to the one British House of Commons. The G.L.C. breaks clear of both these restrictions as it has its own electoral base and its own regional functions, the weakness in this case being the Government's insistence on prescribing precise limits, statutorily defining the division of powers between the two tiers and generally exercising the sort of supervision that used to be thought suitable for an urban district council.

If a new form of regional government is to be set up in Britain, it will be no use trying to pretend that it can be done without sweeping changes of structure and attitude on the part of the existing central government and on the part of the new local authorities and their officials. It will be disastrous if there is an attempt simply to add to some of the plethora of present forms, to try and avoid opposition by extending some of the existing advisory councils, by devising additional regional departments or by inflating the more competent of the present town halls. A reformed system must be explicitly created to meet new needs, a step which will require an essentially conservative community to adopt new methods and attitudes.

Chapter 7
Welsh and Scottish Nationalism

Part of the criticism of the existing framework of local government made in chapter 1 was that the public were increasingly apathetic about elections and about standing for the local councils. Beside the calls for increasing popular participation in decision-making there was a refusal to use the existing democratic machinery. When local citizens were angered by decisions to build an airport at Stansted, to close grammar schools in Bristol or to shut down the Highland railway lines, they formed special organizations and took their protests to the appropriate minister. While more and more matters of importance were being settled by local and regional government agencies, it became harder to get candidates to stand or electors to vote as belief in the efficacy of the existing machinery of government was not strong.

These sentiments, an insistence that government could and should do much more and an almost contemptuous dismissal of the present system, are the leading features of the nationalist movements that sprang into prominence in Wales and Scotland after 1966. For some politicians, the explanation of the Nationalist victories at Carmarthen in 1966 and at Hamilton in 1967 was simply disappointment at the economic failures of the Labour Government; they regarded them as part of a protest movement which would die away either when Labour achieved a reasonable increase in living standards or when a Conservative Government took over and did so. The older

Scottish M.P.s recalled the Scottish Covenant agitation of 1948 to 1950 when two million signed the petition for more devolution, an agitation which faded away during the economic recovery of the early 1950s.

In a sense this analysis accepts the point that the irritation against politicians and the apathy revealed in England springs from the same source as the nationalism in Scotland and Wales, the difference being that in the latter cases there is a plausible explanation and another political party ready to capitalize on this discontent. But it is also possible that the disenchantment with local democracy as it now stands will remain even after economic recovery.

There is evidence that the nationalist leaders in Scotland and Wales were themselves taken by surprise at the sudden expansion and success of their parties and this does raise the problem of how deep and lasting this political force will be, how far Wales and Scotland are nations and whether there is sufficient consciousness of a separate history and tradition to produce steady support for the nationalist parties.

Welsh Nationalism

In the case of Wales, there are traditions and social patterns which might well have produced a nationalist movement at an earlier stage. The governing elements in Wales in the nineteenth century were an English landed gentry and an Anglican church both of which were cut off from the masses who spoke Welsh and attended non-conformist chapels. There were positive attempts to eradicate these distinctively Welsh features, particularly in education where commissions appointed in 1846 declared that 'the language is a vast drawback to Wales and a manifold barrier to the moral progress and commercial prosperity of the people'. At the same time, industrial development was linking South Wales to the industrial midlands of England and bringing in Englishmen to manage the factories and mines.

There was thus a native tradition and a challenge. As education spread, it encouraged local sentiment. An Act of 1889 allowed local councils to levy a rate for secondary schools and their control was given to a purely Welsh body, the Central Welsh Board, in 1896. In 1893, the three colleges at Aberystwyth, Cardiff and Bangor were constituted the University of Wales and a separate Welsh Department was formed inside the Ministry of Education in 1907. At this stage, there was a struggle over devolution, some Welshmen (notably D. Brynmor Jones) wanting a Council of Wales to control education while the Government preferred control by the English Ministry, agreeing under pressure to the separate Welsh Department in London. Nevertheless, the schools did much to discover and encourage a consciousness of Welsh language and tradition. In the mid nineteenth century, there was a revival of Welsh literature, poetry and choral singing encouraged after 1880 by the annual gathering at the National Eisteddfod.

At the same time, the extension of the franchise in 1867 and 1884 brought politics to the Welsh for the first time. With an alien gentry and church, it was natural that they should turn to Gladstonian liberalism and from 1880 Wales became a virtual Liberal preserve. Religion combined with politics on one major objective, the disestablishment and disendowment of the Anglican Church. Other interests were security for tenant farmers, temperance, better industrial conditions and later, opposition to British imperialism.

It is not surprising that when Gladstone turned to Home Rule for Ireland, some of his followers in Wales began to ask why Ireland had a separate executive and a claim to home rule, why Scotland had its own Church, Law, educational system and, from 1885, a special minister, when Wales had none of these things. This view was first put effectively by Thomas

Edward Ellis who stood for Merioneth in 1886 as a Liberal and as a Welsh Nationalist. He formed Cymru Fydd (Wales of the Future) as a society to call for a Welsh Parliament, that is for home rule within the United Kingdom. By the early 1890s, backed by Lloyd George and Alfred Thomas, there were proposals to put a top tier on the county council system in order to consider matters of common interest to Wales, to create a devolved executive for Wales and to appoint a Secretary of State. In 1891 the Liberal Party committed itself to Welsh Disestablishment, Ellis became a junior Whip and Lloyd George urged Home Rule for Wales.

It might have been assumed that if the Liberal Party had continued to have periods in office and had home rule for Ireland been carried, home rule for Wales would follow. But this development was cut across by two connected trends. These were the industrialization of South Wales and the collapse of the Liberal Party. As early as 1898, D. A. Thomas turned the South Wales Liberals against home rule. In this area English was normally spoken, the connexions with London and the Midlands were growing closer and resentments were not over lack of self-government but over industrial conditions.

This was the position at the time of the First World War, a Wales divided between north and south, chiefly interested in disestablishment and social reform where there was a consciousness of being Welsh but with a very different emphasis as between the rural, Welsh-speaking north and the industrial English-speaking valleys of the south. The experiences of the inter-war years confirmed and deepened this division. The slump had a devastating effect with 10 per cent unemployed from 1927 to 1931 and 16 per cent from 1931 to 1936. As well as the 245,000 out of work at the worst stage, 300,000 emigrated. This experience confirmed the doctrine that the real problems were social and class problems. Language and culture were an irrelevance to starving men, the way out being clearly a victory for Labour in Westminster and progress towards social justice. The most powerful Welsh Labour spokesman, Aneurin Bevan, was completely opposed to any talk of nationalism.

The Welsh nationalist movement was thus left to the language enthusiasts from the rural areas. They profited by the activities of the University of Wales, by the spread of adult education, by societies such as the New Wales Union (Undeb Cymru Fydd) and the Welsh League of Youth (Urdd Gobaith Cymru) but all this had little political effect. Once the Anglican Church was disestablished after the First World War, the religious issue began to decline and so did the number of Welsh speakers. In 1925 Plaid Cymru, the Welsh Nationalist Party, was created and soon fell under the leadership of John Saunders Lewis. A literary man, a pacifist and a Catholic, he identified the little party with an intellectual concept of pre-reformation, Welsh-speaking Wales and with the idea that the main solution to Wales's problems was the rejection of English influences. At a time when the mass of his countrymen were desperate to screw a bare subsistence wage out of the employers or the government, this seemed almost entirely irrelevant, as did his gesture of setting fire to an R.A.F. camp in 1936 when the dangers from Germany were proved to be only too real a few years later.

Redemption for Wales came with full employment and higher wages during and after the war. By 1945 most major departments of state had a Welsh office and controller. These together provided material for an annual Report on Government activity in Wales, there was an annual debate on Welsh affairs, and in 1948 an Advisory Council for Wales and Monmouthshire was created. It seemed possible that as the insufficiency problems were solved after the war and as the electorate had more time for and interest in participation in local affairs, there would be progressive devolution at least at an administrative level.

The Conservative Government after 1951 made the Home Secretary also Minister for Wales and in 1957 the Council for Wales recommended a Secretary of State in the Cabinet with a department which would take over housing, local government affairs, planning, health, education and agriculture. The Labour Party responded to this, in part, in 1964 by creating a Secretary of State, but he was allocated only housing, local government, town and country planning, new towns, certain Land Board and civil defence functions, roads and some functions relating to forestry, water resources and national parks. A little later a report was issued on Local Government in Wales (Cmnd. 3340) which was the work of this new Department. The Report recommended that in place of the existing 181 local authorities, there should be three county boroughs (Cardiff, Newport and Swansea) and five amalgamated counties. Beneath these five, there should be a second tier of thirty-six district councils, the division of powers being the same as at present between counties and non-county boroughs. Finally, there was to be a nominated Welsh Council to take over the duties of the Welsh Economic Council, the former Council for Wales, the Welsh Arts Council, the Development Corporation for Wales and the Welsh Tourist Board.

It is no secret that the then Secretary of State for Wales, Mr Cledwyn Hughes, originally proposed an elected Council to perform these functions but was defeated in the Cabinet, a major opponent being Mr William Ross, the Secretary of State for Scotland, who argued that he could no longer resist some form of elected assembly for Scotland if there were such a body in Wales. The failure to carry out the proposals of this White Paper has concealed some inconsistencies among the various lines of devolution being advocated. As regards local government, the White Paper follows the unsatisfactory method of retaining the distinction between town and country, keeping three boroughs as separate bodies; this is the 'line of least resistance' discussed earlier. And if a Council for Wales is to be an effective executive body, either elected or nominated, it should take over some local government powers such as police and fire services and further education. Finally, an effective body of this kind not only makes it unnecessary to expand the office of Secretary of State but might even make it redundant. Elective and administrative devolution cannot be pursued together unless the elected council is left only minor virtually advisory tasks.

While these discussions about devolution were taking place inside the Labour Party and Government, the Nationalists in Wales suddenly increased their strength and became an important factor in Welsh politics for the first time. Having consistently collected an average of 11 per cent of the votes in the seats they contested from 1955 to the general election of April 1966, in July of that year the Plaid Cymru candidate in Carmarthen, Mr Gwynfor Evans, increased his share of the poll from 16 per cent to 39 per cent and captured the seat from Labour. In March 1967 the Welsh nationalist candidate in Rhondda West had a favourable swing of 27 per cent, cutting the Labour majority from 18,888 to 2,206.

What had happened in the brief period since the 1966 general election? Clearly a movement of feelings, perhaps from several sources, had come together and focused on Plaid Cymru. Since 1945, the leader of the party had been Gwynfor Evans, whose chief motive was a desire to preserve the Welsh language and traditions. More popular and practical than John Lewis, he nevertheless still only appealed to a minority mainly in rural Wales. But at the same time, other elements and arguments had begun to appear in the party. Some non-Welsh speakers had joined whose objection was neglect of the Welsh economy and the remoteness of London Government. In particular, it began to be argued that Wales was used, for example, to provide a water catchment area but was given little in return to meet such special problems as the sudden decline in the mining industry. On top of these strands, there came after 1966 a sudden doubt as to whether the Labour Government was capable of renewing Welsh industry, whether (for those in well-paid employment) it was providing the kind of lead and scope for enthusiastic support that the younger people wanted, and finally whether it cared for the distinctively Welsh aspects of life in central and northern Wales. Support for Plaid Cymru was a way of giving vent to these feelings. It is not necessary for a party of protest to have only a single theme or to be entirely consistent. A combination of factors, having brought victory in a single by-election, then helped to build up the Party. Slowly the emphasis on the Welsh language and traditions, instead of being the central theme of the Party, is becoming merely a part of a general resentment at the remoteness and apparent lack of concern of Whitehall.

The question that matters here is how far this nationalist sentiment will continue to be a factor in Welsh politics and how it can and should influence any proposals aimed at providing a satisfactory and lasting system of local government. One effect is almost certain. Several of the large-region solutions based upon suitable areas for economic planning have insisted that Wales is not a single unit. They have argued that the southern section is linked to a Bristol–Severn region, the middle of Wales to Birmingham and the north to Liverpool. Yet an important factor in choosing suitable regions is the degree of sentiment and patriotism they can arouse and whatever else Plaid Cymru and its recent victories has or has not shown, it is undeniable that there is a strong Welsh sentiment which would be bitterly offended if the country was divided and linked in segments to English regions, a sentiment which could provide great backing for an all-Welsh elected government.

This is all that needs to be demonstrated, as the case for such large units of government has already been made. Proposals for devolution to an all-Wales elected authority are likely, however, to be denounced by some of the older Labour M.P.s as dangerous, and by Plaid Cymru as inadequate, but the aim of such proposals would not be to attract votes. The aim would be to produce a sound system of democratic government for Wales which could debate and determine those aspects of domestic policy which can best be settled for Wales as an entity, leaving minor matters to second-tier councils. Only after being in operation for some time would such a series of institutions begin to engage people's loyalties and diminish nationalist support till the demand for total separation was lost in a healthy competition over Welsh affairs and for control of the Welsh Parliament or Assembly.

Scottish Nationalism

Scotland has preserved more of its national institutions than Wales, since the country was not incorporated into England but accepted a Treaty of Union in 1707. The terms of the Treaty left intact the Scottish legal system, a distinctive pattern in local government and education and the established Presbyterian Church of Scotland. While the Scottish aristocracy, including the Highland chiefs, tended in time to educate their sons in England and to lose touch with Scottish life, they also retained a certain pride in their country so that the claim to be a Scotsman was usually treated with reasonable respect by the English upper classes.

With the Scottish bar and appeal courts in Edinburgh keeping a centre for the legal profession in Scotland, with the annual General Assembly of the Church of Scotland acting as a focal point for Scottish opinion and with the four ancient Scottish universities contributing an academic life which enjoyed a European reputation, Edinburgh remained a quasi-capital in a sense that Cardiff never was. But, as in the case of Wales, the lack of national flavour among the aristocracy meant that nineteenth-century Conservatism never took a deep hold in Scotland and the country became a Liberal stronghold from the 1832 Reform Bill until the First World War. This political alignment was strengthened by the struggles over patronage in the Church of Scotland and by the power of both the Free Church and the Free Presbyterian Church.

On the other hand, the Gaelic language was confined to the Highlands and never became identified with Scotland as a unit nor was there any one distinctive culture or dialect or literature that could act as a unifying factor. When Mr Gladstone talked of Home Rule all round, it was more on the grounds that Scotland could not be denied something that was being offered to Ireland, rather than in response to pressure from the Scots. There had been a small movement complaining of under-representation and maladministration in 1853 which reappeared in various mild forms till a Secretary for Scotland was appointed in 1885. Thereafter, as has been described (see p. 111 - above), departments were collected in Edinburgh till a special ministry was formed in 1939. Thus it proved possible to obtain specific reforms if there was pressure, but there was little demand for home rule for Scotland. The Liberal Party in Scotland had split on home rule for Ireland, Scottish sentiments were in many ways strongly British and patriotic and only a few Liberal M.P.s were dissatisfied with the existing system. On the other hand the early Labour M.P.s disliked the Scottish establishment and strongly sympathized with the Irish nationalists, so that most of them were prepared to support home rule and the Rev. James Barr M.P. introduced three private bills to this end in the 1920s. Ramsay Macdonald suggested an inquiry in 1929, but then the slump had the same effect as in Wales. The sheer burden of hunger, unemployment and slum housing convinced all Labour M.P.s that the real objective was power, the defeat of the bosses and the redistribution of wealth, and from this point of view appeals to national feeling were either irrelevant or a positive trap. The Conservatives had always felt themselves part of a single British governing class and the influx of Liberal Unionists after 1886 confirmed them in their view that anything that might lead to a Scottish Parliament would be a disaster. As a result, little was heard of Scottish nationalism from the 1930s onwards.

The Scottish National Party was created in 1934 but attracted little attention (though because of the Party truce during the War, it was able to elect an M.P. for Motherwell for a few months in 1945). A Mr John McCormick founded a non-party 'Scottish Convention' in 1942 which collected two million signatures on a 'Scottish Covenant' calling for more devolution to an elected Scottish assembly in the late 1940s. The Conservative Party, which was busy attacking the alleged over-centralized state socialism of the Labour Government under Mr Attlee, lent some unofficial support to the Covenant. So when returned to office in 1951 the Conservatives had to re-establish the soundness of their unionist position and appointed a Royal Commission on Scottish Affairs under Lord Balfour (Cmnd. 9212). The terms of reference carefully excluded any consideration of the key issue, the value of an elected Scottish assembly. The Royal Commission was charged simply with reviewing existing administrative arrangements and concluded that responsibility for roads, for the appointment of Justices of the Peace and for animal health should be transferred to the Secretary of State.

During the 1950s administrative devolution became as complete as was feasible, given the desire to retain uniform standards in taxation, social security and industrial regulations. The only way in which the duties of the Scottish Office could have been increased would have been by the transfer of the Board of

Trade's responsibilities for the location and assistance of industry. An extra Minister of State was appointed making five in all at the Scottish Office in addition to the two Law Officers. Then, as it became clear that it was possible to speak of a Scottish economy, the features of this economy became identified/as an undue dependence on agriculture and on the declining heavy industries leading to a lower average wage and double the level of unemployment recorded in the U.K. as a whole. By 1959, with the Conservatives losing three seats in Scotland (while winning an overall majority of 100), attention returned to the concept of regional planning and special measures to restore the relative position of the Scottish economy. Starting from the Toothill Report (see pp. 113-16) above, a series of studies documented the problem, the Conservative Governments offered special tax concessions in 'growth points', while the Labour Government declared almost the whole of Scotland a development area and offered direct grants to manufacturing industry and a regional employment premium for all working in industry.

Against this background, the Scottish National Party appeared to be a small squabbling faction of some 2,000 members. Its leadership lacked calibre, its policy consisted of a mixture of complaints that Scottish taxpayers subsidized their English counterparts and the claim that independence would produce greater prosperity. The biggest achievement of the Party had been to capture almost all the Conservative votes in a by-election in West Lothian in 1962, the S.N.P. candidate coming second with 9,750 votes. At the 1964 and 1966 general elections, S.N.P. candidates did better than before but at a relatively low level so that they attracted little public attention.

Then in March 1967, at the Pollok by-election, the S.N.P. came a close third behind the two major parties after a vigorous campaign. In Hamilton, eight months later, Mrs Winifred Ewing turned a Labour majority of 16,576 into an S.N.P.

majority of 1,799, this breakthrough being confirmed at a nation-wide level by the local elections in May 1968. At these elections the total of votes cast in the four major Scottish cities was:

	Conservatives	Scottish National Party	Labour
Edinburgh	53,825	49,119	27,969
Aberdeen	19,314	15,508	14,971
Dundee	22,962	18,452	18,050
Glasgow	93,269	96,913	68,605
Total	189,370	179,992	129,595

This constitutes an unprecedentedly rapid breakthrough for a third party and one which, as in the case of Plaid Cymru, seems to have taken the S.N.P. itself almost by surprise. What then are the reasons for this and what effect should it have on any proposals to recast the pattern of local democratic government?

The first point is to make some estimate of who the nationalists are. Surveys have been carried out in Glasgow, Hamilton and Dundee. All suggest that the active S.N.P. members (there are 115,000 in 448 branches) are relatively new to politics, 85 per cent of their candidates in Glasgow having never belonged to any other party and 80 per cent having joined the S.N.P. only in 1967 or 1968. It is also clear that in these areas, the S.N.P. voters tend to be in the younger age groups in Glasgow (nine years younger on average than other party supporters), mainly Protestant and roughly equally divided between male and female. The Dundee survey shows that in terms of class, the S.N.P. gets its support almost equally from skilled manual, unskilled and miscellaneous trades, the interesting point being that it has two per cent higher support than Labour among the skilled workers. The impression the party creates also varies with the nature of the constituency, all these polls having been taken in urban areas where Labour is the normal majority party. There is some evidence that in Liberal-held seats the S.N.P. takes more support from them and tends to be a lower middle class party, the same being true of Conservative-held seats. But in the areas surveyed the preponderant switch is from Labour, 33 per cent in Glasgow and 35 per cent in Dundee of former Labour votes having moved over to the nationalists. All the polls suggest a total voting strength of between 25 and 35 per cent of the community.

The rush towards the nationalists is hard to analyse in terms of policies and motives. Clearly there have been underlying trends in Scottish politics which the combination of circumstances in 1968 have brought to the fore. The poll material on the subject is not clear, though all the indications are that only a small group in the electorate actually favours the S.N.P. policy of total independence and quite a considerable percentage (on the Dundee poll) of S.N.P. voters do not think the party in fact wants or stands for total independence. The *Glasgow Herald* reported the answers to a question about how Scotland should be governed:

No change 14 per cent
Complete independence 21 per cent
Some Home Rule but remain in U.K. 38 per cent
Greater local and regional freedom 27 per cent

Surveys in Craigton and Hamilton both confirmed that a majority of the electorate wanted devolution to an elected body in Scotland but only a small minority were in favour of independence. The Hamilton answers supported the view that a majority of S.N.P. voters did not accept the policy of total separation but thought this was the best way of pushing the major parties into some activity.

Looking at the broader lines of propaganda employed by the S.N.P., the importance of their constitutional proposals seems to decline. The general assumption is that Scotland could be a much more prosperous place, whether on its own or better governed as part of the U.K., and that the citizen does not get any proper return for the taxation he pays or any adequate control over a remote and indifferent government. All this is combined with a mixture of envy and dislike of the more confident and cosmopolitan stereotype upper-class Englishman who may well seem to act as a barrier to full recognition or promotion. Unless this emotional mixture of resentment at existing frustrations and desire for a simple explanation for current discontents is appreciated, some of the propaganda of the S.N.P. appears ridiculous.

For instance, there is the constant theme that Scotland subsidizes England. This is inherently unlikely since in no other country with uniform rates of taxation is it suggested that the poorer areas subsidize the richer. On modern systems of taxation an area pays in rough proportion to the incomes of its citizens and the profits of companies based there. In Scotland wages and salaries are lower than in England and most wealthy firms have their headquarters in London. As a result it is not surprising that Scotland contributes less than its share to the national Exchequer. At the same time modern states pay out most of their money on education and social welfare and here Scotland has more than its share of unemployment, sickness, bad housing and (for traditional reasons) a higher proportion of children going into Colleges of Further Education and into Universities. Thus Scotland both pays less into and receives more than its share out of the national Exchequer. Evidence of a similar situation is provided by Northern Ireland. It was supposed under the 1920 Act to pay the same taxes, to receive the same benefits and out of the margin to pay an 'imperial contribution' towards the cost of defence and foreign policy.

By the late 1920s it was appreciated that as a poor region with a greater need for social benefits there was no margin left, and even when the requirement for an 'imperial contribution' was waived the United Kingdom Treasury had to go further and provide a direct subsidy for Northern Ireland. The Scottish Nationalists counter such reasoning by saying that Scotland loses proportionately on the non-apportioned elements (which in 1965–6 amounted to £59 5s 1d a head) such as defence expenditure, as there are so few bases in Scotland and so little research is commissioned north of the border. But this ignores both the small proportion of defence expenditure and the fact that if Scotland was independent no such moneys would be forthcoming. Even if sheltering behind England and NATO, Scotland would have to make some further expenditure on her own defence.

Indeed, far from being sacrificed, there is much evidence that Scotland (quite rightly) gets specially favoured treatment. Because the Conservatives were alarmed at their weaknesses in Scotland and because Labour owed its 1964 majority to its specially strong hold there, all Cabinets have given way to demands for special treatment by Secretaries of State for Scotland.

This evidence that Scotland is better off in every case except libraries and museums, police and fire services, is simply not believed by S.N.P. spokesmen and members. The strength of their disbelief lies in the fact that if an independent Scotland did not have more money (or even had less) for its services, the S.N.P. would have to argue that some sacrifices were involved and it would have to produce its own list of priorities. A great deal of the success of S.N.P. propaganda arises from the irritation felt against both the Labour and Conservative Parties for disappointing the electorate's expectations of increasing easy prosperity. Nationalist leaders can avoid any similar taint by arguing that there would be no recessions, no wage freezes and

Revenue (Net Receipt) 1952–3 (Cmnd. 9051) (Scotland's population is 9·7 per cent of the total for Great Britain)

	As collected				As adjusted to give true contribution			
	In England & Wales	In Scotland	From other Sources*	Total	By England & Wales	By Scotland	From other Sources*	Total
	£000	£000	£000	£000	£000	£000	£000	£000
Income Tax	1,604,060	113,576	18,597	1,736,233	1,537,226	155,379	43,628	1,736,233
Surtax	131,200	—	—	131,200	117,968	11,164	2,068	131,200
Death Duties	135,262	16,588	—	151,850	132,901	16,396	2,553	151,850
Stamps	46,438	3,812	—	50,250	44,041	5,212	997	50,250
Profits Tax and Excess Profits Tax	345,821	26,659	3,620	376,100	320,686	42,373	13,041	376,100
Excess Profits Levy	2,604	336	10	2,950	2,408	459	83	2,950
Special Contribution and other Inland Revenue Duties	1,988	32	—	2,020	1,788	134	98	2,020
Customs	913,453	70,109	40,936	1,024,498	903,288	99,023	22,187	1,024,498
Excise	665,601	70,283	3,209	739,093	662,380	69,375	7,338	739,093
Motor Vehicle Duties	62,088	5,570	—	67,658	62,088	5,570	—	67,658
Total Revenue from Taxes	3,908,515	306,965	66,372	4,281,852	3,784,774	405,085	91,993	4,281,852

	As collected				As adjusted to give true contribution			
	In England & Wales	In Scotland	From other Sources*	Total	By England & Wales	By Scotland	From other Sources*	Total
Broadcast Receiving Licences	13,382	1,200	218	14,800	13,382	1,200	218	14,800
Receipts from Sundry Loans	—	—	24,681	24,681	—	—	24,681	24,681
Miscellaneous	19,245	3,409	94,728	117,382	19,245	3,409	94,728	117,382
Total Non-Tax Revenue	32,627	4,609	119,627	156,863	32,627	4,609	119,627	158,863
Total Revenue	3,941,142	311,574	185,999	4,438,715	3,817,401	409,694	211,620	4,438,715
Per cent	88·79	7·02	4·19	100·00	86·00	9·23	4·77	100·00

*The figures in these columns include the produce of the reserved taxes in Northern Ireland services and payments in respect of the Northern Ireland residuary share of these taxes.

Expenditure Per Head of Population 1966–7

	Total Public Expenditure		Central Government Expenditure	
	Scotland	England and Wales	Scotland	England and Wales
	£ s. d.	£ s. d.	£ s. d.	£ s. d.
Roads (including Lighting)	9 19 11	8 4 10	6 6 0	4 8 2
Airports	12 9	7 8	12 9	4 1
Ports	16 7	12 4	5 —	
S.E.T. Additional Payments	13 1	15 9	13 1	15 9
Promotion of Local Employment	3 12 1	9 3	3 12 1	9 3
Agricultural Support	6 6 0	4 0 7	6 6 0	4 0 7
Agriculture and Fishery Services	1 19 4	13 7	1 19 4	12 0
Forestry	11 2	1 7	11 2	1 7
Housing	32 15 9	16 10 4	4 12 1	1 18 4
Environmental Services	15 10 11	12 11 8	15 0	10 7
Libraries and Museums	11 11	1 3 8	2 4	4 10
Police	4 4 4	4 16 6	1 18 11	2 2 5
Prisons	13 1	11 9	13 1	11 9
Other Law and Order (including Fire Services)	1 17 0	2 6 2	15 10	17 8
Education (excluding Universities etc.)	31 14 11	27 15 4	3 10 2	1 5 3
Universities and C.A.T.s	7 3 9	4 16 2	7 3 4	3 17 5
Health and Welfare	30 1 1	27 2 1	27 3 3	23 2 0
Children's Services	7 5 8	6 10 2	6 6 0	5 11 5
Benefits and Assistance	47 13 11	44 14 6	47 13 11	44 14 6
General Rate Deficiency and Equalization and Transitional Grants to Local Revenues, etc.	—	—	24 15 1	22 3 2

Central Government Expenditure 1966-7

	£ million		Column (2) as percentage of Great Britain total
	England and Wales (1)	Scotland (2)	(3)
Roads (including Lighting)	212	33	13
Airports	10	3	23
S.E.T. Additional Payments	38	3	7
Promotion of Local Employment	22	19	46
Agricultural Support	193	33	14
Agriculture and Fisheries Services	29	10	26
Forestry	4	3	43
Housing	92	24	21
Environmental Services	25	4	14
Libraries and Museums, etc.	12	—	5
Police	102	10	9
Prisons	29	3	9
Other Law and Order (including Fire Services)	43	4	9
Education (excluding Universities and C.A.T.s)	61	18	23
Universities and C.A.T.s	187	37	17
Health and Welfare	1,111	141	11
Children's Services	268	33	11
Social Security	2,150	248	10
General Rate Deficiency and Equalization and Transitional Grants to Local Revenues, etc.	1,065	129	11
Other Services, etc.	—	15	—

no credit restrictions in an independent Scotland. This is not a cultural nationalism (though poets and scholars are members) willing to face hardship in order to preserve its identity. On the other hand it is not purely material in that a sudden revival of British economic prosperity would not end the movement. Many of its members are young and have not only never known unemployment but are better off than previous generations.

Partly just because the old quantitative problems of too few jobs and houses, too low wages and living standards, have lost their edge, these younger electors are becoming more interested in qualitative aspects of life. They share the feeling that government is remote, complex and hard to influence, and this can easily be translated into the view that government is far off and must therefore be administered by Englishmen in London. To reply by pointing out that many important functions are administered by Scotsmen in Edinburgh makes little difference: some do not comprehend the point and those that do are not affected by the knowledge.

While there is no unifying cultural theme to S.N.P. propaganda, there is a pride in a general feeling of 'being Scottish' and a resentment at ignorance or condescension from the southerner with an Oxford accent. To appreciate this, one has only to put together such reactions as that of a Scots Brigadier to the remark 'Oh, you're from Haggis-land!', that of a Glasgow M.P. to the editor of a left wing weekly who said 'there's no one capable of first rate work in Scotland; if there was he'd be in London', and that of a workman in a pub who asked an English visitor for a light in a Scottish accent and was told 'what a perfect example of Jock-speak!'

Thus the S.N.P. have managed to catch a vague feeling that expectations have been raised and disappointed, that government is remote and unconcerned, and that the character and outlook of the Scots are not properly respected, all of which can be combined in the proposition that the existing system of government is unsatisfactory.

On the issues being examined in this book there are some lessons to be learned. The most obvious is that administrative devolution in no way assuages such discontents. The existence of the Scottish Office has had no effect in reducing or preventing the rise of nationalist feeling. Only an elected assembly or Parliament which had powers to debate and decide Scottish matters would meet this desire for greater involvement and local control.

It may be argued that it is essentially unrealistic to expect an elected Parliament with no greater amount of money to spend and with the same (very able) advisers to produce new and much more satisfying answers to, say, the Highland problem or the clearance of the Glasgow slums. But this is the traditional objection to any subordinate territory receiving a measure of self-government. There is a value in doing the job oneself, in hearing the arguments and in allowing local pressure groups to hear their case being put and answered. This is, after all, the case for democratic local government, whose value is so often praised in Britain. But if it is true for the citizens of Liverpool or Lancashire, it is surely also true for the Scots or the Welsh, particularly when they have made it evident that such group or national consciousness is a very real sentiment.

Chapter 8
Meeting the
Nationalist Case

Some politicians, particularly in the established parties, argue
that precisely because there is some strength behind the
nationalist arguments, they should be resisted. It is sensible,
according to them, to grant some degree of self-government to
a group of counties or a conurbation where no local loyalties
exist and there is no pressure for devolution, but it must be
resisted precisely in those cases where there is such a demand.
This apparently paradoxical and undemocratic view rests on
two arguments. The first is that to grant a measure of self-
government, even to give county council powers to an elected
Welsh or Scottish assembly, would be to whet the appetite of
the nationalists who would demand more and more till total
separation became inevitable.

This argument has no evidence to support it and most
modern experience indicates the contrary. There are no historical cases of a degree of devolution being used and exploited
to lead to total independence. On the other hand, existing
federations all find that the member states are unhappy about
paying for the most expensive services or find their boundaries
unsuitable for some purposes and so the central government is
asked to resume or increase its range of activities. It is the refusal to grant a measure of self-government when it is ardently
desired that is most likely to lead to increasing pressure and
more extensive demands for autonomy. The best example is
Ireland where the 1886 Home Rule Bill, had it been passed,

might well have satisfied all Irish desires for internal self-government and kept Ireland part of the United Kingdom. It was the blind refusal of the Unionists to pass any of the three Home Rule Bills and then the mishandling of Anglo-Irish relations in the First World War which destroyed the old Irish Nationalist Party and its programme of internal home rule and led to the rise of Sinn Fein with its demand for complete independence. The poll evidence cited in the previous chapter shows that something similar is happening in Scotland at present. The majority of those voting S.N.P. do not favour total independence, but because the established parties have refused any concessions (until a recent Conservative offer) the sixty-five per cent in Glasgow who want some devolution to an elected assembly have had no choice, if they wish to express their feelings, except to support the nationalists.

The second argument is less often explicitly advanced but is very strong. It is claimed that elected assemblies in Wales and Scotland, while not wishing for more autonomy, would nevertheless have such positive public support behind them that they would create centres of power capable, on some issues, of standing up to Whitehall and of rivalling Westminster. A Prime Minister of Wales (or of London and the South-East) would have at least as much weight as a junior Cabinet minister. Whitehall's concept of reformed local authorities is one of efficient units but not of bodies with political power capable of pursuing independent policies on some issues and of bringing strong pressure to bear on the central government. Many M.P.s, particularly as it happens from Scotland and Wales, are primarily interested in local affairs and some of them would be very unhappy if such matters as housing, health and education were being determined in Cardiff or Edinburgh and if, on these matters, another elected representative had a larger role to play than they had in the House of Commons.

But this is the issue. Is Britain to remain as completely

centralized in its decision-making as it is to-day? If not, then the consequences of creating other bodies with some real freedom of action must be accepted. It may be the case that many of the nationalists' arguments are false but if they are dissatisfied with the present system this is sufficient reason in itself for a change. If they are ignorant of the current methods of administration, this shows that in a sense government *is* too remote, and if they fail to appreciate the economic benefits of remaining part of the United Kingdom, this proves that the existing level of communication and of participation is inadequate. It is possible for individuals to disagree with the views of large sections of the electorate, but it is dangerous and undemocratic to refuse either to respect these views or to attempt to meet them if they persist.

The Grand Committees

One possible approach that has been canvassed is to allow the Welsh and Scottish Grand Committees to meet in Cardiff and in Edinburgh. At present these Committees sit in the mornings at Westminster and take the second readings of bills that affect only Wales or Scotland. They meet (in the case of the Scottish Grand Committee which is the more active) six times on the Scottish estimates when the Opposition choose the topic and on two 'subject days' when the Government selects the topic. The result is some twelve or fourteen meetings a year for the Scottish Committee and four for the Welsh.

The Committees consist of all Welsh or Scottish members with sufficient English M.P.s added to produce an equivalent to the party balance in the House itself. This is, however, scarcely necessary as there can be no division in the Committees since in each case the procedure takes the form of a report to the House of Commons. Normally the Committees meet at

10.30 a.m. and open with a front bench speech on each side; some five or six backbenchers are called and then a front bench speaker winds up for the Government and for the Opposition, the debate closing at 1 p.m.

This arrangement has met with little criticism from Welsh Members, but Scottish M.P.s have often complained that two and a half hours to cover such topics as education, agriculture or housing is quite inadequate, and that only half a dozen out of the forty or fifty who attend are able to contribute. Mr David Steel, the Liberal M.P. for Roxburgh, Selkirk and Peebles, has elaborated on these criticisms in his pamphlet *Out of Control*. He has pointed out that the Secretary of State for Scotland has responsibilities covered by nine English Ministers, and while English M.P.s can therefore spread their constituency questions over nine days, Scottish M.P.s have only the one chance every six weeks when the Secretary of State comes to the top of the rota system for answering questions.

It would be possible to remedy these defects and make some concession to the arguments that Westminster government is too remote and that its existing concern for Scotland is too little known, if the Grant Committee met in Edinburgh. As no divisions are possible, there would be no need to import the balancing number of English members. Meetings could take place for the last week of the summer recess, for a few days at the end of the Christmas or Easter recesses and for a week at Whitsun. Thus Scottish Members would not be denied any of their rights or time in the House of Commons. The procedure might start with a Scottish question time followed by a debate in which all who wanted to speak could take part, and each day could end with an adjournment debate on a constituency problem. Meeting in the recess when there was no other political news would ensure excellent local publicity.

But though this proposal has certain attractions, it would not meet the problem of providing either proper democratic control or an independent executive in Scotland. The chief weakness is that a Secretary of State could not be held responsible to a Grand Committee whether there was any voting or not. The Minister is a member of the U.K. Cabinet and has to accept its decisions on policy. He could not alter or amend his ideas to meet the views put forward by M.P.s in Edinburgh or Cardiff. In the most extreme case, there might be the problem of a Labour majority in Wales and probably in Scotland, at the same time as a Conservative Government was in power in Westminster. Debate is important as it helps to inform both the public and ministers but debate without any chance of affecting the course of events is stultifying and would soon lead to pointed criticism. All the weaknesses of a regional administration described in chapter 6 above would remain in that it would be impossible to pursue policies with variations to meet local needs when the ultimate responsibility lay with the Cabinet and the House of Commons. Finally, this would not remove the weaknesses of the existing pattern of local government. To create new local authorities within Scotland and Wales and to give them larger and more effective powers would go far to reduce the work of the Scottish and Welsh Offices and therefore the topics open to discussion by the Grand Committees. On the other hand, to retain the Scottish Office with its present powers (and to confer the same on the Welsh Office) would leave relatively little for independent decision by any new and stronger pattern of local government. Thus while this proposal might help to produce better discussion of Scottish and Welsh affairs in an interim period before local government reform (or regional devolution) has been prepared and carried through, it is in no way a long-term solution of any of the problems presented by either the administrative or the political aspects of Scottish and Welsh government.

Mr Heath's Assembly

A variant of this proposal was put forward by the Leader of the Conservative Party on 18 May 1968, under the somewhat high-flown title of 'The Declaration of Perth'. Mr Heath called for an elected Scottish Assembly to 'take part in legislation in conjunction with Parliament'. The object was to permit purely Scottish legislation to be handled at certain stages in Scotland; there would be 'a direct link with the Secretary of State for Scotland ... as well as with Parliament' and the Assembly would 'provide co-ordination on those matters where it is required, including finance and capital expenditure' between the new local authorities and the central government.

Such vague statements could be interpreted in many ways but however they were applied, the objections to such a scheme would be powerful. The most obvious stumbling block is the same as arises in the case of the Grand Committee sitting in Scotland. A separately elected assembly (which would probably contain a Labour plus Nationalist plus Liberal majority over the Conservatives) would have more authority than the Grand Committee if it took a separate stand on any matter. Yet once such an Assembly was denied the right to propose or reject measures, it would be denounced as a farce. If, on the other hand, it could introduce, amend or reject bills, there would be the fiercest resentment at any suggestion that these proposals could then be reversed by an English-dominated House of Commons. The fact is that one set of Ministers cannot be held responsible to two different elected chambers whose political composition is most unlikely to be exactly the same. Moreover, Ministers would not be in the Assembly to propose or defend their measures. Finally, it is hard to imagine how such a body could co-ordinate local authority work when it might differ from the government over priorities.

In all, this proposal is utterly vague and ill-defined, though in any form that would fit the general prospectus given by Mr Heath it would exacerbate rather than assuage Scottish separatist feelings.

Federalism

It is because of the impossibility of having one executive responsible to two elected houses that many have been attracted by the idea of a federal solution. Federalism is based on the assumption that it is possible to make a fairly clean cut through the mass of governmental functions and to divide the powers of taxation, awarding one part to the state and the other to the federal government. But there are grave difficulties in any such scheme and these are best illustrated by an examination of recent federal plans or bills that have been put forward.

In November 1966 Mr Russell Johnston, the Liberal M.P. for Inverness, brought in a Scottish Self-Government Bill. It proposed a single-chamber Scots Parliament of seventy-one members elected by the existing constituencies with powers to legislate on all matters of 'internal government', while seventy-one other members from the same constituencies went to Westminster with no right to speak or vote on questions 'relating exclusively to England, Wales or Northern Ireland'. All taxes except customs and excise were to be levied by the Scottish Parliament and paid into a Scottish Treasury. Internal services would be paid for by this Treasury while the Scottish contribution to U.K. services would be paid for partly by the Scottish Treasury and partly by the U.K. Treasury in proportions to be agreed by a Joint Exchequer Board. The Scottish executive would be responsible to the Scottish Parliament for all matters except the Crown, foreign affairs, defence, customs and excise, currency, 'and such economic policy as is agreed to affect both countries'. For these functions there would be a U.K. executive responsible to the U.K. Parliament.

In March 1967 Mr Emlyn Hooson, the Liberal Member for Montgomery, introduced a Government of Wales Bill, the same Bill being brought in seven months later in the House of Lords by Lord Ogmore. This Bill, though a little more elaborate, was on essentially the same lines as Mr Johnston's. The Parliament of Wales was to have two members from each of the existing constituencies (seventy-two in all) and subjects excluded from its competence were the same as in the case of the Scottish Bill except that the list included lighthouses, submarine cables, wireless telegraphs, postal services, weights and measures, marriage and divorce, and the judicial committee of the Privy Council. A clause provided for religious, racial and linguistic equality in Wales, while U.K. laws were to be paramount but only in those matters reserved to the U.K. Parliament. Subsequent clauses allocated all taxation to the Welsh Parliament except income tax, surtax and capital gains taxes. A Joint Exchequer Board would determine the amount of these 'reserved taxes' paid into the U.K. Treasury and the share of this to be used for U.K. functions, the rest being paid back to the Welsh Exchequer. Some details of judicial powers, appeals, the transfer of powers and the position of the civil service were set out and a schedule apportioned National Debt charges and the cost of the Civil List.

In 1968 the *Scotsman* declared in favour of federalism as the best response to the desire for more self-government in Wales and Scotland and published its plans in a pamphlet entitled *How Scotland should be Governed*. England, Wales, Scotland and Northern Ireland should, it argued, all become sovereign states within a federation. The Federal Parliament would deal with the Crown, foreign affairs, defence, weights and measures, currency, the balance of payments, monetary policy, banking, overseas trade, customs and excise. The nationalized industries would have to be divided to give Scotland control of its transport, fuel sources and industrial policy. In the federal parliament 'a paramount need is to ensure adequate representation to Scotland, Wales and Northern Ireland in order to counter-balance the overwhelming numerical superiority of the English . . . . One chamber in which English members cannot outvote the combined opposition of Scotland, Wales and Northern Ireland is desirable', and the U.K. legislature should meet in York. The pamphlet was vague, not to say muddled, on questions of taxation and economic policy, the only definite conclusion being that Scotland should pay a proportion of her Gross National Product into the Federal Exchequer. This was peculiar since customs and excise and monetary policy were left to the Federal Government but there was no attempt at precision in the argument. It included some quite contradictory statements such as that 'there would be joint committees, properly representative of each country, to supervise such matters as monetary policy and the balance of payments' when a few pages earlier monetary policy and the balance of payments had been assigned to the Federal Government. (Quite how a joint committee could undertake the present duties of the Treasury, the D.E.A., the Board of Trade, the Bank of England and the Commissioners of Customs and Excise was not explained.)

These three proposals are clearly more in the nature of declarations of intention rather than any serious attempt to work out the problems of a federal system under modern conditions. If the authors are tempted to reply that they were not concerned with marginal matters of technique, the answer is that the present system, though much criticized, is not intolerable. It needs changing but it would be foolish to proceed without a carefully elaborated alternative which gives some promise of meeting the current criticisms and of not setting up other equally annoying frustrations or anomalies.

Accepting that Messrs Johnston and Hooson and the *Scotsman* want some sort of federal system, it is better to examine the proposals for such a system when they were seriously worked out in 1886, 1893 and 1912 and to see how the culmination of these Home Rule Bills for Ireland, the Government of Ireland Act of 1920, has actually operated in the one area in which it was tried, Northern Ireland. Not only does this permit an empirical test in the case of Northern Ireland, but the Liberal Party Bills for Scotland and Wales just described were, in fact, much abbreviated versions of the old Home Rule Bills of the nineteenth century.

The three Home Rule Bills and the Government of Ireland Act were all based on a few, relatively simple, assumptions and they encountered the same intractable problems even at the early stage of passage through Parliament. The first assumption was that certain 'imperial functions' could be isolated and left with the Westminster Parliament while 'internal matters' could be transferred to Dublin (or Belfast). This was a more sensible idea eighty years ago, when there was not the vast range of central government activity that there is to-day, but even in 1886 it caused difficulties. In addition to the Crown, defence, foreign affairs and religious establishments, the 1886 Bill excluded trade and navigation, taxation of trade, coinage and legal tender, weights and measures and the Post Office. The Irish critics saw at once that this excluded three-quarters of the Irish revenue. It also prevented the creation of a tariff barrier, the only method then known of aiding agriculture, Ireland's main industry. In 1893 Gladstone set out the principle of 'one system of legislation for all the Kingdom on commercial affairs', but held that it was enough for Westminster to control customs and excise and postage rates. (The time when income tax was to be used for social purposes was not then foreseen, much less the resort to purchase taxes, credit control and deficit financing.) By the time of the Third Home Rule Bill in 1912 government was becoming more complex and this was reflected in the Bill. Besides the powers kept for the U.K. Parliament in the earlier bills, Asquith also reserved for British control certain services, particularly those set up under the Old Age Pensions and National Insurance Acts, and spelled out the U.K. Parliament's power of concurrent legislation over the subjects left to Irish administration. All taxes imposed by the U.K. Parliament continued to be paid in Ireland, but the Irish Parliament was allowed to lower the rates of these taxes provided the sum to be transferred to the Irish Exchequer was reduced by an equal sum. All taxes, except postage, whether levied by the U.K. or Irish Parliaments, were to be paid into the British Exchequer. A similar system was adopted in the 1920 Act.

The second assumption which proved to be difficult to translate into practice was that the revenue arising in Ireland or paid by Irish taxpayers could be identified and restored to them and that the Irish share of U.K. or 'imperial charges' could also be estimated. In 1886 Gladstone felt that customs and excise had to be fixed and levied by the U.K. Parliament. Then on various tests he calculated that Ireland's fair proportion of imperial charges was one fifteenth. Irish expenses thus amounted to the civil costs in Ireland plus one fifteenth of the U.K.'s Annual Debt charge plus the same fraction of the cost of the army, navy and such U.K. civil charges as were determined as imperial. After subtracting these charges, the British Exchequer would return the customs and excise profits; in 1886 this left a surplus of £404,000. A special Exchequer Court was set up to settle disputes and readjust the fraction to be paid by Ireland. Parnell and his Party felt that the imperial charges were too heavy so the 1893 Bill reduced the fraction to one twentieth. But instead of paying this, Ireland simply handed over the proceeds of the customs duties (which equalled about one twentieth of the charges) as an imperial contribution, keeping the rest of the tax revenue to defray Irish expenses. Britain was to pay a third of the cost of the Royal Irish Constabulary and the result left Ireland a surplus of £500,000 a year. Because of criticism from both the Irish and the Unionists, this plan was completely altered in committee. The final Bill threw out the customs revenue scheme and went back to calculating the imperial contribution as a fraction of imperial charges. Also provision was made for a special levy on the Irish in time of war.

By 1912 an Irish surplus of £2 million had become a deficit of £1·5 million, so that there was no question of Ireland making a contribution to imperial expenses. Instead, as explained above, Britain collected all taxes and granted Ireland sums of money to cover Irish services and administration. A Joint Exchequer Board replaced the Exchequer Court to settle contentious points and revise the arrangements (including an imperial contribution) once Ireland again had a surplus. By the time the 1920 Bill was introduced, Ireland did have such a surplus so her contribution was fixed at three per cent of imperial charges. The U.K. levied all 'reserved' taxes on customs and excise, incomes and profits, handing over what was left after the three per cent was paid. This was then added to the taxes Ireland could collect on her own – death duties, stamp duties and certain types of licensing.

The third constant difficulty was representation. Some taxes and some powers were left to the U.K. Parliament; how was Ireland to have fair representation there? The first idea was to give up having members at Westminster for though matters affecting Ireland would be settled there Gladstone said 'it passes the wit of man' to define such imperial occasions. Also the executive required a fixed majority and this could be imperilled if Irish M.P.s were sometimes present and sometimes not. The Irish agreed that they needed to concentrate on internal problems and did not want to come and be second class citizens at Westminster. But there was so much criticism of this exclusion that Gladstone was offering to give way when the Bill was lost. As a result, in the 1893 Bill, the Irish were to be represented by eighty M.P.s (the correct proportion) and be allowed to vote on Irish issues. This again led to such difficulties that it was abandoned at committee stage in favour of allowing them to vote on all subjects. The same solution was adopted in 1912 but Irish representation was cut to one M.P. for every 100,000 people which with 4 university M.P.s made 46 in all. The 1920 Act followed the same lines, the inclusion of 4 university M.P.s giving Northern Ireland 13 M.P.s to the South's 33.

Some of the present advocates of federalism, while accepting the intricacies of dividing functions and taxation, may feel that this problem will not arise if all four countries are represented in a federal parliament. But it cannot be brushed aside easily. A federal parliament chosen in proportion to population would give England forty-five out of every fifty-five seats and it is quite unrealistic for the *Scotsman* to imagine that the English would consent to a chamber with effective power in which the ten million Scots, Welsh and Irish had as many or more members than the forty-five million English. The English Parliament would, in fact, dominate any Federal Parliament and the problem of dividing the proceeds of taxation would be exacerbated in that it would constantly come up in the form: 'how far will the English have to subsidize their hangers-on in the coming year?'

The Stormont Model

All three difficulties mentioned have remained in the case of the one experiment in federalism tried in Britain, the Northern Irish Government and its relations with the British Government. It is useful to consider how these relations have developed in order to see where matters stand in the 1960s, whether any mistakes in the 1920 Act could have been avoided and how far 'the Stormont Model' might meet the demands for more self-government in the English regions and in Scotland and Wales.

After 1920, the major problem lay in Northern Ireland's relative poverty and in the concept explained above that under a federal system the member states should 'live off their own', that is, pay for themselves out of their own revenue and contribute a fair share towards the common costs. The system was that Irish taxes then brought in about a tenth of the Irish revenue. The rest came from 'reserved taxes' levied at uniform rates for the whole U.K. This money was collected in London, and after Northern Ireland's contribution to imperial services had been deducted the rest was paid to the Government in Belfast. As first calculated, over half the money went on common services, and Northern Ireland, with a falling revenue and a desperate need for proper services, was faced with a deficit.

The problem was reviewed between 1923 and 1925 and it was agreed that taxation should be uniform and that Northern Ireland must provide some services for its citizens. The implication was that the imperial contribution must come down and perhaps even disappear, a situation which the British Government did not accept but which began to look likely in the 1920s. After some discussion, an 'equalization payment' was offered by the British Exchequer in return for some Treasury control over the Unemployment Fund. Even then the problem grew worse in the slump but the Northern Irish Government adopted every expedient rather than offer lower pensions or unemployment relief than was current in Britain. London, for its part, forced Stormont to revalue and raise more money in rates. By the later 1930s the financial situation improved and during the war a different and better atmosphere prevailed.

In 1945 the situation was stabilized. It was assumed that Northern Ireland would provide 'parity of services' with Britain and in return any expenditure which rose above the British level or which raised important issues would be submitted to the Treasury in London. When National Insurance was introduced in Britain in 1948, the Northern Irish Fund was amalgamated with the British Fund and the Treasury promised help if the cost of the social services was proportionately more in Northern Ireland than in Britain.

The result, from the point of view of the Government of Northern Ireland, is fairly clear. Each year the Ministry of Finance has to guess at the level of taxation to be imposed and the revenue to be received by the British Exchequer. As Stormont gets the fixed percentage of 2·5 per cent of whatever is raised, either buoyancy due to good trade or an increase in taxation (for defence or in order to cause a deflation) all bring more revenue to Northern Ireland. At the same time the Ministry knows that the Treasury must, by convention or gentleman's agreement, approve any expenditure above British levels, but it is assumed that the provision of services and payments equal to those offered in Britain is a first charge on Irish revenues. As a result the imperial contribution remains but is a kind of shock-absorber which can be allowed to fall in a bad year (in 1967–8 to half a million pounds). If it fell any lower the Ministry of Finance in Belfast would have to resort to such expedients as borrowing and the imposition of stringent reductions on the spending departments. The net result of the

1920 Act as it is now (1968) operated in financial terms is that Northern Ireland gets approximately £187 million from the Exchequer in London, £23 million from Selective Employment Tax transferred, and raises £10·5 million on taxes allotted to the Stormont Government. Treasury control is almost as effective as over any Whitehall Ministry and though there is room for experiment and special levels of payment, these have to be justified and perhaps economies have to be offered in other fields of expenditure. The cornerstone of the system is that despite being a poorer, more remote area with a backlog of neglect to make up, Northern Ireland enjoys the same standard of services and endures no greater taxation than the rest of the U.K.

Looking at the other aspects of government policy, there has been the same tendency for developments to leave the 1920 Act and its careful apportionment of powers behind. For instance, agriculture was supposed to have been left entirely to Stormont. In fact, Britain wanted the maximum agricultural production during the Second World War and was prepared to pay for it, while the farmers wanted to share in the higher prices being offered. As a result, after the 1947 Agricultural Act, the guaranteed prices and production grants were extended by agreement to Northern Ireland. A chief official of the Ministry of Agriculture goes to London each year and plays a full part in the Annual Price Review. In 1967–8 £27 million of British taxpayers' money was spent on agricultural support in Northern Ireland while under the 1957 Act a further £1·75 million is awarded each year to compensate for transport costs, that is for the remoteness of the country. Compared with these figures, the Stormont Ministry spent £10·3 million of its own money on research, advisory services and marketing. The same fishing subsidies and grants are payable in Northern Ireland and the Egg and Wool Marketing Boards cover that area, as do the White Fish Authority and the Herring

Industry Board. Any special expenditure, even of the locally raised £10·3 million, is checked by the Treasury but special needs can be met. Northern Ireland has its own Pig Board and Seed Potato Board and can give its sanction to farm improvement schemes and offer technical advice more rapidly and with more local knowledge than is possible in Britain.

Education in Northern Ireland has had the special features of serious neglect in the past and the need to reach an accommodation with the Roman Catholic hierarchy. The result has been some particular adaptations to local situations and an overall effort to catch up with developments in Britain. Thus the 1944 Education Act in England was followed by a similar Northern Irish Act in 1947, though it took till 1957 to raise the school leaving age to fifteen. On the religious issue, the Government put up its offer from covering 65 per cent of the running costs of voluntary schools to 95 per cent provided local authority representatives were accepted on the boards of management and the Roman Catholic Church agreed. The Ministry feels (as do the Cabinet) that, where personal benefits are concerned, it would lead to discontent and emigration if the position was clearly less satisfactory than in Britain. So when British students all received grants once they were accepted by universities, Stormont decided to follow suit. The rates of grant were different for a while, but were brought into line in 1963. Similarly teachers' salaries keep pace with any increases granted in Britain. On the other hand, in institutional matters the Northern Irish Ministry feels free to go its own way and make arrangements for voluntary schools in a manner that fits the Irish situation and to stand aside from the whole move towards comprehensive schooling being pushed through by the English ministry.

The same kind of balance could be illustrated in every field. In commerce, for instance, the Northern Irish Government offered grants to incoming firms five years before this policy was adopted in Britain and when Whitehall followed suit the Stormont Ministry felt they had to keep a slightly higher rate of grant. Also the speed of decision and personal attention the Northern Irish ministries can offer is a positive asset in attracting industrialists. The Health Service in Ireland is organized in a manner which suits local conditions and avoids some of the weaknesses of the English and Scottish counterpart. There have even, at times, been efforts to adapt social service payments, an unsuccessful attempt being made at one stage to alter family allowances so as to penalize large families.

This survey of the federal experiment in Northern Ireland clarifies certain points. In the first place, the notion that an element of devolution must lead to an immediate rush towards total separation is a false one. Some commentators would explain this fact and indeed most of Northern Irish policy by reference to the Unionist Party's determination to stick as close as possible to Britain and to follow British policies 'step by step'. But there are other equally potent forces pressing in the same direction. Poorer areas simply cannot keep up the same standard of services without either paying higher taxes or becoming more dependent on their richer neighbours. The experience of a measure of self-government shows those concerned how dependent they are on aid from the centre where the largest taxable resources and sources of investment are concentrated. Also the sea channel is narrow and Northern Irish farmers, students, unemployed, businessmen and those needing medical treatment would all raise a tremendous clamour if the various levels of provision were not up to those available in Britain. So whether Stormont was controlled by the Unionists or not, the pressure for a high degree of uniformity and co-operation would remain.

The second lesson is that the room for manoeuvre by small countries closely tied to large rich neighbours is small. Given that popular demand would insist on no higher taxes and no lower standard of services, the scope for regional variations of policy is small. On the other hand, though Northern Ireland never wanted to be forced into Home Rule, it must be accepted that the system has become popular. Very, very few in the country would wish to give up the experiment now and become a totally integrated part of Britain once again. M.P.s at Stormont are better known than the twelve who go to Westminster and few can deny that the House and the Government have real vigour and receive strong support from the community.

The final point is that the old nineteenth-century (and current Liberal) attempts to create easy federal divisions of functions and of taxes just will not work. The division is no longer between an external function such as defence and purely internal regulations. Most functions have economic and external repercussions or cost money which affects financial relations with Britain, but this does not mean that it is not possible or desirable to carry out these functions with regional variations. As regards taxes, it is often extremely difficult to track down the source of the goods or income, so that territorial divisions of revenue are hard to establish and, in view of the tendency of money earned in the regions to appear as profits on the books of a London-based firm, the results can be very unfair. While a measure of financial autonomy is desirable for local and regional governments, a key decision in politics is how much of the takings of the nation and its wealth-centres is to be distributed to each of the various regions. Far from regretting, as some commentators do, that regionalism or the case of Northern Ireland brings this question out into the open, the proper response is to welcome the fact that such important issues are at least being discussed and that pressure groups in the form of regional elected assemblies or parliaments exist to see that an answer is produced.

Eire

Lest the more ardent nationalists think it possible to evade the dilemmas Northern Ireland has had to face simply by a flight into total independence, it is useful to note the experience of Eire. After a series of arguments culminating in a new constitution in 1937, Professor Chubb still feels that 'what is surprising is not the differences' as compared with the British system of government 'but the similarities in form and fact . . . in the distribution of functions, the forms of administrative organization, the structure and professional standards of the civil service, the pattern of local authorities, and even parliamentary procedure'. The distinctive features are the provisions for a referendum, the articles setting out personal rights, the use of forms of proportional representation and the tendency to cut down the powers of elected local government councils.

However the central question is how far Eire has had a genuine independence and has been able to act independently in a manner which has not been possible for Northern Ireland because of its ties with Britain. The answer is that the freedom available to a small country, the vast majority of whose trade is with a single large neighbour, is extremely limited. It is possible to choose not to trade or allow foreign capital to control native firms but the result is to choose stagnation. In the dispute known as 'the Economic War' with Britain in the 1930s (over payments due under the old land purchase legislation) each side put on import duties, Irish trade fell sharply and agricultural wages sank to a level of between eight and twelve shillings a week. Insistence on a certain amount of the capital of any firm operating in Ireland being held by Irishmen also frustrated economic development so that by the end of the 1930s poverty was acute. In the first generation after independence 800,000 of the four million Irish citizens emigrated.

The alternative policies which gathered way in the 1950s and culminated in the Anglo-Irish Free Trade Agreement of 1965 brought increased prosperity, though the Irish average weekly wage in manufacturing industry was still only £11 9s. compared with £20 16s. in the U.K. But the revival of trade and investment from outside means closer links particularly with Britain. The Irish money market is entirely tied to London and the two currencies are interchangeable, so that Ireland in practice has no choice on such matters as devaluation or entry to the Common Market or decimalization. If Britain decides to act on any of these questions, Ireland must do likewise at once. In 1966 and 1967 the Irish rate of growth has remained at a reasonable level despite cut backs in Britain, but on the whole the Irish economy is so closely associated with that of Britain that rates of activity and consumer price levels have tended to coincide since the last war.

There is no attempt here to weigh the other alleged benefits of total independence. Material needs are not everything. Undoubtedly Eire is poorer as a result of independence with farm incomes lower than in Northern Ireland (which enjoys British guaranteed agricultural prices), with no health service and with compulsory free secondary education only being introduced in 1968. It is hard to say whether total independence has produced a compensating increased sense of dignity and of nationhood or whether Irish cultural life is richer than in the years before the First World War. Ireland has a voice in international affairs but what matters in these spheres is not so much a country's voice as its weight. Apart from a few situations where impartial small nations are asked to chair committees at the United Nations or send peace-keeping detachments to troubled areas, their foreign influence is negligible. This is certainly the case with Eire; its world role seems to have little interest for its citizens and sometimes a year passes without a debate on foreign affairs in the Dail.

Irish citizens may resent any discussion of their policies since the rise of Sinn Fein and the establishment of the Republic, but they cannot blame Scotsmen and Welshmen who are being urged to act in the same manner asking whether it has all been worth while. The point is that simply declaring independent a small country, which in Scotland's case has over 80 per cent of its trade with a large neighbour, does not solve all problems. Such an action will almost certainly decrease prosperity, it may hasten emigration, it will not stop the pull of London or New York circles for local actors, authors, painters or scientists, and the effect on the outlook of the community is hard to calculate. On the other hand, there are aspects of policies which ought to be determined locally, where, however able the regional civil servants, the people want to play their part in making the decisions. There is a virtue, when government does so much, in having centres of decision close to the local communities so that government is rapid, open and humane. The problem being discussed in this book is whether the Scots, the Welsh, Londoners or Yorkshiremen can have it both ways. Is it possible to construct a system of government which fits modern society so that citizens can exercise some control over the events that affect them? If so, it would seem that this control is best exercised at the several levels at which decisions can be grouped and effectively taken, one being at the immediate local level for minor amenities, the second being at the regional level where many important policies are made or applied and the third being at the national level. (In time, for Britain, there may be a higher grouping on a European scale for some decisions).

The mistake made by the Nationalists is that they imagine that all this can be done at one level only. It may be true that in Eire (or in Scotland or Wales) a parliament has so little to do and the scale is so small that it can normally take over the duties of second-tier local government councils. But the same parliament cannot also have complete freedom in handling major economic policies, which are also the business of fifty million other people close at hand, unless it decides on a policy of self-sufficiency and accepts the resultant poverty. British unionist politicians may have been so blind and so arrogant and so much damage may have been done to Irish pride that by 1920 there was no honourable solution but independence. Yet this was unfortunate because the various attempts at Home Rule (though couched in what is now an old-fashioned and unsuitable federal form) would have enabled the Irish to get the best of both worlds, to govern themselves from Dublin and to participate in the wider decisions in London. In addition the U.K. would have benefited by their continuing stimulus and vitality. It is to be hoped that the opportunities for such a sensible and mutually beneficial solution to the problems of democratic reform and national feeling are not lost again through inflexibility and narrowness on the part of our present political leaders.

Chapter 9
Conclusions:
A Workable Regionalism
for England, Scotland
and Wales

The problem of government outside Whitehall has now been examined from both ends, from that of local government reform designed to produce a more democratic and effective series of local councils, and from the opposite end, the need to devolve central government powers, and the most promising solution to emerge takes the form of elected regional councils. These could both be the top tier of a new system of local government and be large enough to undertake regional planning, transport, the preservation of the countryside, and similar essentially local functions at present left to nominated bodies or the central government. Such regional elected councils, perhaps with a few extra powers, could permit all the regional variations of policy and the local control which are a feature of the Stormont system in Northern Ireland, while at the same time meeting the legitimate aspirations of the Welsh and the Scots for a degree of self-government and for jurisdiction over those aspects of policy peculiar to their own countries in a manner which would avoid both the retrograde step of total separation and the unnecessary complications of a formal federal system.

The object of this chapter is to sketch the outlines of such a regional solution and to discuss those aspects of the internal management, staffing and electoral system which have not so far been considered. Once again, it is necessary to start with the areas of the top-tier councils.

Nine English Regions, Scotland and Wales

In order to remove all 'intermediate government', to have regional planning supervised by an elected body and to make a degree of devolution of central powers possible, a series of large regions is the most satisfactory solution. The nationalist challenge in Scotland and Wales makes a number of valid points, of which the most obvious is that these two countries must be treated as units and not split up in any way. The one boundary change that would be desirable would be to include Berwick-on-Tweed in Scotland as it is the outlet of the Tweed Valley for planning purposes and is neglected at the moment, being regarded as a remote northern outpost of the Northern Region. For six further regions the boundaries of the present economic planning regions meet the maximum number of needs; they are the Northern, North Western, Yorkshire and Humberside, West Midlands, East Midlands, and East Anglia regions.

The three difficult areas are the boundaries of the South-West, the treatment of the region around London and the residual territory in the Bristol-Oxford-Southampton-Bournemouth quadrilateral between the core of the South-West and the environs of Greater London. In the case of the South-West the problem is that the sentiments and interests of Devon and Cornwall plus parts of Somerset and Dorset are distinct and could in time have a certain unity, while Plymouth could be accepted as the administrative centre of such a region. Bristol (the present location of the South-West Planning Council) is far away and has a quite different area of interests around Severnside. The multiplicity of boundaries already in this area (see map on p. 189) shows the difficulty administrators have had in solving this problem. It may be unfortunate to add yet another division but if Bristol and its

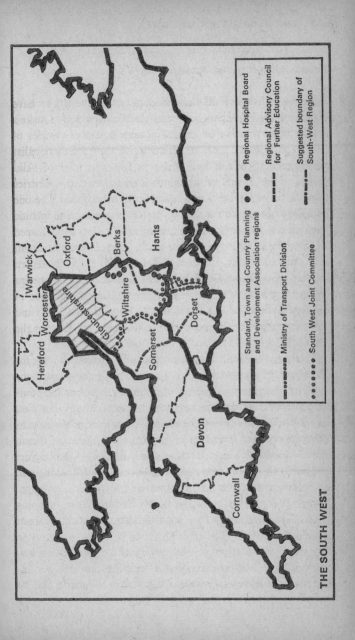

THE SOUTH WEST

Legend:

— Standard, Town and Country Planning and Development Association regions

••• Regional Hospital Board

–·– Ministry of Transport Division

– – – Regional Advisory Council for Further Education

••••• South West Joint Committee

—··— Suggested boundary of South-West Region

Counties labelled on map: Warwick, Hereford Worcester, Oxford, Berks, Hants, Gloucestershire, Wiltshire, Somerset, Dorset, Devon, Cornwall environs are to be excluded, this removes Bath and the north-eastern section of Somerset, while the eastern sections of Dorset around Poole are much more closely connected to Bournemouth and Southampton. As a result it would be most suitable to draw the boundary through Somerset and Dorset as indicated on the map in order to create a reasonably homogenous unit whose inhabitants could all think of themselves as belonging to the South-West.

As for the London and South-Eastern area, the Greater London Group of the London School of Economics was unable to come to an agreed conclusion. Some of its members wanted a single regional authority while others preferred a division into the G.L.C. plus four surrounding regions each of about two million people. The choice between them depended entirely on the issue which has always lain at the centre of the dispute between the city region (or amalgamated county) supporters and the advocates of the large regions: whether economic planning, the allocation of land, the planning of the communications network and the public transport system are to be regional or central government tasks. It has been argued here that the opportunity to discuss and settle these questions is one of the principal matters of interest to electors and must be devolved if local democracy is to have real life. As a result, the South-East must be treated as a single region reaching to the borders of East Anglia (north of Essex) in the north, including Bedfordshire, Hertfordshire, Buckinghamshire, the south-east of Oxfordshire and Berkshire around Reading and the north-east corner of Hampshire. This (see map on p. 191) includes virtually all the South-East which in any way looks to London and whose communications network cannot avoid London.

While these divisions create reasonable South-Western and South-Eastern regions, they leave behind a residual area including Bristol with its surrounding zone of influence, Oxford

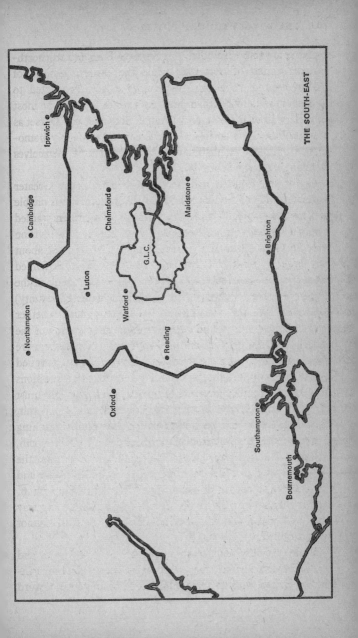

THE SOUTH-EAST

PROPOSED ELEVEN REGIONS

which has London as well as western connections, and the main Channel ports of Southampton and Portsmouth. Such a region has no unity but all these cities would be equally unhappy if they were forced into neighbouring regions centred on Plymouth or London, while to divide the area into a Severn Region and a Southampton Region would produce two abnormally small units compared with the other regions. As a result, while recognizing that none of these solutions is entirely satisfactory, this area might be best treated as a single unit.

The result of these divisions is to produce nine top-tier regional units in England, which, with Scotland and Wales, would give a total of eleven governments, all of considerable power in terms of population and resources, and able to manage extensive functions and engage staff of the same quality as the central civil service.

Functions and Second-Tier Units

The Regional Councils in England and the Elected Assemblies in Scotland and Wales would be responsible for the following functions:

Regional planning (including planning of major communications)
Highways (construction, maintenance)
Housing (large scale redevelopment, overspill, new towns)
Agriculture (advisory services, marketing, research)
Forestry
Fishing (grants and loans, supervision and research)
Countryside amenities (parks, preservation of coasts)
Police
Fire services
Water supplies
River pollution (flood control)

Education (higher, further and in some cases secondary)
Refuse disposal
Regional transport
Support for the Arts
Main drainage
Hospitals (preventive medicine, G.P. and welfare services)
General competence (to do anything not prohibited by law which might be in the interests of electors)

The problem of the appropriate size and powers for second-tier units becomes almost unmanageable if an attempt is made to produce a uniform system for the whole of the U.K. Such uniformity is quite unnecessary and, given the different densities of population in different parts of the country, quite undesirable. In the case of the South-East and possibly also of the East and West Midlands and the North-West, it might suit local conditions to have large second-tier units of 200,000 to 500,000 capable of major local government functions. Where the population is highly concentrated, such second-tier councils could be both local and effective. But in the more rural regions or in Scotland, Wales or East Anglia, second-tier units containing this number of people would be far too large and would cover vast tracts of territory ignoring all local feelings and traditions. In Scotland, for instance, it would be highly desirable for the Borders to be a single unit and almost essential for Orkney and Shetland each to have their own second-tier unit. In such cases, the regional council or elected assembly would have to undertake more than the functions listed above. This has been found to be desirable in Northern Ireland where the total population of 1·5 million is served by six county and two county borough councils which are, for all practical purposes, second-tier units. But because of their lack of resources, the Stormont Government has kept a number of functions which are normally given to county councils or to county boroughs in England, such as police, fire services, youth employment, aspects of housing and public transport. The Northern Irish pattern in this respect would be entirely suitable for the South-West, Scotland, Wales, East Anglia and the Northern Region. Indeed, it is not necessary for all second-tier authorities within the one region to have the same powers, the units suitable for the Newcastle-Sunderland-Durham complex being too large for the Lake District or northern Northumberland.

The arrangement of second-tier sizes and functions is a matter which would require re-adjustment in the light of experience and population changes and should not be laid down by the central government. Thus a further responsibility which ought to be given to the regional councils would be to devise and regulate the pattern and powers of second-tier local government in their own regions. Also the two-tier system should be genuine in that all control of the second-tier should be with the regional councils – financial controls, boundary changes, staff supervision (if any is needed) and any appeals on planning or other decisions.

With this arrangement, the sort of tasks which regions such as the South-East or West Midlands might delegate to large and rich second-tier units would be:

Planning: implementing sub-regional plans
Secondary roads, traffic management, road safety
Housing construction and management
Education: primary, perhaps secondary
Children's services
Libraries
Refuse collection
Public Health (shared with regions)
Regulatory functions, shops, weights and measures
Local sewerage
Local amenities

In more remote or rural areas where the second-tier authorities might be much weaker in terms of population and resources, planning and secondary roads might have to be reduced in scope, and secondary education and the children's services removed, but the readjustments could be made, as has been said, to suit each particular situation.

In this scheme, Scotland and Wales, like Northern Ireland, would have substantially the same powers as the English regions. To those who argue indignantly that these parts of Britain are counties or nations rather than regions, no insult is intended. The point is that the aspects of Scottish and Welsh life that are national will be revealed in the character and quality of the services provided and the atmosphere created by the elected assemblies. More powers could be granted but there is no point in doing so if the Scottish and Welsh assemblies would, as Stormont has done, simply prefer to have matters where uniform standards are clearly desirable (e.g. agricultural subsidies) or where the cost is too great (atomic research) handed back to the U.K. Parliament. But there are some responsibilities which could and should be added, over and above the powers to be given to the English regions, particularly in the case of Scotland where there are other separate national institutions which are entirely manageable by a five million strong community. The most obvious is control over the Scottish legal system, law courts, prisons and all Home Office functions except immigration and passport control. Similarly Scotland and Wales should have powers to organize and stimulate tourism whereas there is little point in having nine separate tourist agencies and campaigns in England.

The method by which these responsibilities are granted by the U.K. Parliament should be an improvement on the formal federalism attempted in the various Home Rule Bills. It is unsuitable in modern times to try and allocate functions in their entirety, because there is a real popular pressure for uniformity of standards in some fields and the extent of this demand may alter rapidly. For instance in education the most appropriate method would be for the U.K. Parliament to pass an Act declaring that all state education must be free, compulsory to a certain age, and that certain minimum standards of pay and qualifications for teachers must be maintained. Thereafter, the regional councils would be empowered to organize and run all aspects of education, making, where necessary, subordinate legislation for their own region. There is widespread irritation today (even among Scottish and Welsh Nationalists) if qualifications earned in one part of the country are not acceptable to others. It seems likely that, whether Britain enters the Common Market or not, there will be pressure for standardization of qualifications and the U.K. Parliament must be in a position to pass an amending Bill declaring that certain examination results will be accepted as appropriate qualifications to fit in with certain European equivalents.

Similarly in agriculture the central legislation would reserve the major lines of import control and price guarantees for Westminster and leave the rest of the field to the regional councils. The latter could award extra production grants for horticulture, crofters or upland sheep farmers; they could run advisory services and study methods of farm improvement in their areas. Such an arrangement would be desirable largely because this is what the public want. With the Anglo-Irish free trade agreement spreading the impact of British farm prices into independent Eire, it would be foolish to try and cut the present system into eleven different patterns of support. And if a European agreement is reached on a standard price for a product or a uniform grading scheme for agricultural exports, it is desirable that the U.K. Parliament should be able to implement this at once by legislation. But none of this detracts from the need for varied aid for the highly varied conditions in different types of farming country and from the advantage of having inspectors and advisers who deal with a limited area and can specialize in its problems and respond rapidly to any calls.

Under this system the precise margins of the retained powers in Westminster and the responsibilities granted to the regions would not be fixed, but this accords with reality; there is a constant need for marginal alterations and it avoids the fictions now evident in Northern Ireland where the same result is produced by Stormont copying British decisions or agreeing to act as an agency for a British ministry. To apply the pattern of devolved responsibilities the regions would pass subordinate legislation and if they used the powers listed here there would be real scope for regional variations, for making the atmosphere and quality of life in the South-West quite different from that of East Anglia and for the Scots and Welsh to develop their own traditions and look after their special needs, while all the regions would retain the advantage of being for other purposes part of the U.K. and perhaps, in time, part of a united Europe.

Elections

The regional councils and Scottish and Welsh assemblies should be directly elected for a fixed term of three years. There may be a temptation for those worried about a radical change to want to form the second-tier units on a statutory basis with elections and then have an indirect election to large regional councils which would be weak, semi-advisory bodies capable only of working alongside regional divisions of central government departments. This would be a miserable and pointless compromise. If large regions are to be selected as the top tier, then the history of the planning councils shows how unsatisfactory nominated advisory bodies at this level can be. Regions with any strength, with the right to say they represent the people and the authority to execute policies and argue with the central government, must be directly elected. And since the second-tier authorities should be of varying sizes and have different responsibilities according to the nature of the territory, they would not be suitable as the first stage in an indirect election to the regional councils, even if this were desirable on other grounds.

Thus elections should be direct and take place at regular fixed intervals. The number of electors in each constituency would have to vary, as the smaller regions would still require a council of reasonable size. It is possible that the Stormont Parliament with forty-eight members for 1·5 million people is too small a body from which to choose ministers and very small assemblies would become unstable if one or two members became ill and by-elections were pending. Thus chambers of 100 to 150 members would probably be most suitable and this would mean different sizes of constituency in different parts of the country. While elections would have to be held on the register used for parliamentary elections, it would be undesirable to have exactly the same constituencies. No M.P. would want to be working in harness with a regional member for precisely the same constituency, so it would be preferable if boundaries were redrawn for regional elections.

With the kind of powers envisaged here, the incentive for able men to stand as candidates would be far greater than is the case at present in local government. If (as will be argued below) the committee system is abolished, members would have to attend meetings for perhaps a total of two and a half months in each year, though the periods of meeting would be scattered through the year. (The Dail meets on average seventy-five days a year). Thus members would be expected to retain their normal occupations but they should be paid a salary sufficient to be a proper compensation for earnings lost. Members' expenses should also be covered in terms of an allowance for accommodation, travel, postage and secretarial work, to avoid the present problems of M.P.s who are in the invidious position of having to pay more out of their own pockets the harder they work for their constituents.

The Executive

There is a case for an independently elected executive for each of the regions, a Governor of the kind elected for each state in the U.S.A. Such a person would have a very strong position and be able both to speak for the region and to represent its views to the central government. But however cogent the case, the system would only work with a total rearrangement of the relations between the executive and the assemblies on lines unfamiliar to British politicians. For this reason, and because the Prime-Ministerial system, given a secure majority, confers great power on the holder of the office, the normal practice in this country is to be preferred. It is essential, in view of its debilitating effects, that the committee system in local government should be swept aside. Governments as large and complex as those to be created in the regions cannot be run by groups of elected members deciding both policy and administrative detail.

Thus the executive must be a prime minister and cabinet, the latter consisting of about eight ministers, a possible division of portfolios being development, finance, health, housing, agriculture, education, police and fire services, and the arts and amenities. Ministers, unlike members, would have to be full-time and be paid a proper salary.

Staff

For some of those interested in regional government, this has been a major stumbling block. As has been argued above, the G.L.C. is showing signs of the difficulty of running a regional government for eight or nine million people with a staff whose experience was gained in the confined departments of the old town halls. One of the arguments against giving executive powers to elected regional councils is that officials of the necessary calibre simply cannot be found.

But it would be the greatest of errors to prejudice the whole recasting of government outside Whitehall because there was not at present enough talent in the local council staffs to make a real reform work. The correct order is the reverse. If there are important posts offering genuine scope and if the recruitment is pitched at the right level, the manpower will be forthcoming. Once again, Northern Ireland provides the answer. It recruits on the same basis and with the same methods as the home civil service. As a result, a civil service for 1·5 million people has men of the same quality as the Scottish Office or the major Whitehall Departments, while the G.L.C. or Lancashire County Council cannot make quite the same claim, though the numbers they govern are greater than the population of Northern Ireland. This is not surprising for though Stormont has very limited functions, it has much more self-respect and freedom to act than the largest of the present local authorities. The regional governments could do equally well if they decided to recruit and pay their staff on the same basis as the central civil service and if there were easy transfer and secondment between Whitehall and the regional services.

While this should be the long-term pattern, the period immediately after the formation of the new councils will also be important, as there will be difficult transitional stages. It is essential to remove undue fears of insecurity on the part of the ablest officials in local government and also to find sufficient men of drive and experience to head the new regional ministries. This is no problem in the case of Scotland and Wales because the core of the services can come from the Scottish and Welsh Offices, and in the case of the English regions the solution would be a combination of secondment from the civil service and appointment of the best local authority heads of services (all other local authority employees would have to be promised posts at equivalent salaries in the regional or second-tier governments). Any objection that the central civil service could not spare senior men can be countered by the fact that the arrangements proposed here would mean a drastic reduction in the work of the Ministries of Health, Education, Agriculture, Housing and the Roads division of the Ministry of Transport. Indeed a major objective in creating regional government is to reorganize British administration so that the main approach (in internal affairs) is not through a series of vertical subject departments covering the entire country but through horizontal groupings of departments for each region. This will not succeed if there is not a significant reduction in the manpower and activities of a number of Whitehall Ministries and the dispersal of these officials among the regional ministries.

Thus while each region should recruit its own service, so that regional loyalties would develop and the object of an able man's ambition would be to head his own service, it would be desirable that there should be equivalence of ranks and pay so that training could be provided in common for all regional and the central civil services and that crosspostings and transfers between the regional and central services could be easy and frequent.

It follows from these arrangements that the Scottish and Welsh Offices would cease to exist in their present form as part of the central civil service. There would likewise be no need for Secretaries of State for Scotland and for Wales, as their functions in the executive field would be taken over by the Scottish and Welsh Prime Ministries and Cabinets. No case could be made for two of the eleven units in Britain having a special minister in Cabinet, especially when he had no work to do.

Relations between the regional governments and the central government would have to be watched over by one central department, just as the Home Office is now responsible for general dealings with the Stormont Government. This could be managed by a Ministry of the Interior, but there would inevitably be direct dealings between Whitehall departments and their opposite numbers in the regions.

There does not, therefore, seem to be any reason for deviating from the most desirable pattern of reform because of staff considerations, though it will be important both to set the right tone from the start and to reassure those at present in local government that none of them will lose security or salary in the course of the reconstruction of the system.

Finance

As has been argued in the discussion of federalism, the idea that the product of a modern taxation system can be related to given subsections of a country is both difficult and undesirable. It is difficult because companies operating throughout Britain can and often do have their headquarters in London. It is undesirable because regionally differentiated levels of taxation are a constant temptation for people to move (for the wrong reasons), and for regions to undercut each other in the attempt, for instance, to attract new or foreign investment.

The major objectives of any new system of local government finance can be stated fairly easily. The first is to diminish the reliance upon property rating so as to remove its present unsatisfactory aspects. (This tax could be left in large part to cover the diminished functions of the second-tier units, but valuation for rates and the collection of the tax should be a function of the regional government.) The second guide-line would be that it is wasteful and complex to have two sets of machinery for tax collection in each part of the country; it is better to have all taxes collected by the central government and then shared out among the regions. In such a share-out there should be two elements, a flat rate sum per head and an equalizing grant to make up for special problems. Recognized problems would be a low level of wealth per head and special needs in terms of roads, schools or houses. Finally it is desirable for each region to have a certain amount of money, a special tax or source of revenue, on which it could draw if there were special expenditures which it wished to undertake.

In the case of Northern Ireland, the transferred taxes (mainly motor vehicle and death duties) have not provided a fund for special projects, the cost of which could not be met from money supplied by Britain. This need has been met by the so-called 'imperial contribution' which can be reduced if there are special calls on the Exchequer. There is no reason why motor vehicle and even petrol duties should not be collected in and retained by the regions but it would be hard to vary them without affecting industrial costs. Also variations are easier across a strip of sea than within England and it would not be difficult for haulage firms in the Midlands to choose their regional headquarters in order to minimize their tax liabilities. On the whole, the best solution would probably be to have uniform rates for all these items and for the central government to divide the sums it is prepared to allocate for regional services among the regions on the principles suggested. The special fund to cover contingencies, special needs and to cushion changes in the amounts the central government could afford, could come from a surcharge on personal income tax. Mr A. L. Imrie and Mr L. S. Murphy conducted a survey of the Swedish local income tax for the Royal Institute of Public Administration (published as *New Sources of Local Revenue* in 1956). They showed that it is perfectly feasible to add a small amount to the standard rate, have it collected by the existing

Inland Revenue machinery and returned to the area in which the taxpayers lived. It would not be intended to raise much money this way. There might be a fixed ceiling of 3d or 6d in the £ and the purpose would be to provide an extra fund for the 'general competence' function mentioned above. A fund raised in this way would make the political issue of whether electors were prepared to pay for the extra services very clear. If it is objected that this would place an unfair burden upon personal incomes, redress is possible by increasing slightly the rateable value of commercial and industrial premises.

The objection that a taxation system of this kind leaves too much power with the central government raises two points. The first is that, with a need for uniform taxes and a tendency for wealth to drift to the capital in any country, Whitehall has all the most buoyant sources of revenue and what matters in the long run is to have sufficient money available for services rather than a smaller sum raised locally. The second is that the collection of funds is a central problem of modern government. At present all the arguments (long and tendentious each year) are between departments and the Treasury, because that is how British Government is organized. What is proposed here is that, for a large proportion of expenditure, negotiations should be between the regions and the Treasury, and that there is nothing wrong with annual negotiations on an issue of this kind. What is essential, however, is that Treasury control should be kept to a minimum and that regional governments should be free to transfer resources from one branch of expenditure to another. Treasury control has gone too far in Northern Ireland because the assumption that a region could and should pay for its services out of its own resources led to the idea that the country was being specially subsidized. If there was this element of subsidy (which is sometimes put at £50–£60 million a year) it could be argued that it was fair to permit the Treasury to scrutinize all expenditure which seemed high by British standards. But the stigma was unfair. A proper system of taxation and expenditure in any country should ensure that more is raised in the richer areas and more is spent where needs are greater, and there is no need to suggest that this is a weakness which justifies close Treasury supervision.

The system of regional government proposed here would require the regions of England, Scotland and Wales to meet certain minimum standards such as free compulsory education to a certain age, a free health service, certain levels of pay for certain employees and so on. Once these obligations were fulfilled, the rest of the money available to the region could be spent as the council or assembly (and its electors) felt was desirable. There should be no Treasury control over specific projects or items, and sanction for borrowing should be limited to the need to remain within an overall figure set by Treasury. The regions might care to open their books to inspection or to explain future projects in more detail at the annual negotiation about the coming year's equalization grant, but this would be for the region itself to determine.

An arrangement of this kind would keep the financial system of the country as simple as possible. The preparation of the annual estimates and budget proposals and the conduct of overall economic policy would remain the Treasury's responsibility, as would the overall level of internal expenditure, but the way in which this money was spent would be left to the regional governments. Largely free (apart from minimum standards in basic services) from Treasury control, they would be able to determine their own priorities and to ask their electors whether they wanted more spent on roads, say, at the expense of new schools. They would have a special added levy on income tax under their sole control should they wish to raise money for some particular project or contingency not covered by their existing funds. This arrangement is a simplified and realistic version of what federalism has come to be in practice in the U.S.A., Australia and Germany and would provide the regions with the maximum autonomy possible in a country which has (and this includes Eire) an economy and financial system directed from one central point.

Conclusion

A book of this kind which is examining a particular problem and proposing a definite solution faces two dangers. The practical men in central government and the local authorities may say it is too abstract, too theoretical, or that there is too much about democracy and participation which no one understands. The academics and journalists may react in the opposite way and say that there is too much detailed material about boundaries and functions while the overall concepts are not fully worked out.

But the real problem is both intensely practical and a vital matter of theory. The Royal Commissions on Local Government are to report in December 1968 or early in 1969. If the Reports are wrong or muddled or timid, or if they are correct and courageous but are not implemented by the Government, it will be a disaster – a disaster not for any vague reasons of theory but because of the damage that will be done if local government is incapable of organizing our economic growth in terms of factories, houses, water supplies and roads, if the motives that underlie Scottish and Welsh nationalism are misunderstood or ignored, and if we are incapable of reaffirming the democratic element in our tradition. The recasting of Britain's local government system presents as great a challenge as the current need to readjust to a new European role in defence and foreign policy or to restructure the economy to enable it to succeed in a new and competitive trading environment. It is a challenge to take the necessary decisions and carry them through.